Bald

WOMEN BEWARE WOMEN

D1051512

By Howard Barker

Stage Plays

Cheek
No One Was Saved
Alpha Alpha
Edward, The Final Days
Stripwell
Claw
The Love of a Good Man
Fair Slaughter
That Good Between Us
The Hang of the Gaol
The Loud Boy's Life
Birth on a Hard Shoulder
Crimes in Hot Countries
No End of Blame
Victory
The Power of the Dog
A Passion in Six Days
Downchild
The Castle

TV Plays

Cows
Mutinies
Prowling Offensive
Conrod
Heroes of Labour
Russia
Credentials of a Sympathizer
All Bleeding
Heaven
Pity in History

Radio Plays

One Afternoon on the 63rd Level of the North Face of the Pyramid of Cheops the Great
Henry V in Two Parts
Herman with Millie and Mick
Scenes from an Execution

Poetry

Don't Exaggerate; Desire and Abuse

PLAYSCRIPT 111

WOMEN BEWARE WOMEN

Thomas Middleton
and
Howard Barker

JOHN CALDER : LONDON
RIVERRUN PRESS : NEW YORK

First published in Great Britain, 1986, by
John Calder (Publishers) Ltd
18 Brewer Street, London W1R 4AS

and in the United States of America, 1986, by
Riverrun Press Inc
1170 Broadway, New York, NY 10001

Copyright © Howard Barker 1986

All performing rights in this play are strictly reserved and application for performance should be made to:

Judy Daish Associates Ltd
83 Eastbourne Mews, London W6 6LQ

No performance of this play may be given unless a licence has been obtained prior to rehearsal.

ALL RIGHTS RESERVED

British Library Cataloguing in Publication Data

    Middleton, Thomas
     Women beware women.
     I. Title   II.Barker, Howard
     822'.3   PR2714.W6

     ISBN 0-7145-4087-0

Library of Congress Catalog Number

No part of this publication may be reproduced, stored in a retrieval system, or transmitted in any form or by any means electronic, mechanical, photocopying, recording or otherwise, without the prior written permission of the copyright owner and publisher.

Any paperback edition of this book is sold subject to the condition that it shall not, by way of trade, be lent, resold, hired out, or otherwise disposed of, without the publisher's consent, in any form of binding or cover other than that in which it is published.

Word-processed for Photo-typesetting in Boldface by Richard Bates, London
Printed in Great Britain by Hillman Printers (Frome), Somerset

CHARACTERS

DUKE OF FLORENCE
LORD CARDINAL
FABRITIO   Father to Isabella
HIPPOLITO   Brother to Fabritio
GUARDIANO   Uncle to the Ward
THE WARD   The rich young heir
LEANTIO   A factor, husband to Bianca
SORDIDO   The Ward's man
LIVIA   Sister to Fabritio
ISABELLA   Niece to Livia
BIANCA   Leantio's wife
THE WIDOW   Leantio's mother

CITIZENS
MESSENGER
SERVANTS

The Scene

FLORENCE

PART ONE

Scene One

LEANTIO, with BIANCA and MOTHER.

MOTHER.   Thy sight was never yet more precious to me! Welcome, with all
the affection of a mother, that comfort can express from natural love!
Since thy birth joy, thou wast not more dear to me than this hour presents
thee to my heart!
LEANTIO.   Alas, poor affectionate soul, how her joys speak to me! I have
observed it often, and I know it is the fortune commonly of knavish
children to have the loving'st mothers.
MOTHER.   What's this gentlewoman?
LEANTIO.   Oh, you have named the most undervalued'st purchase, that youth
of man had ever knowledge of! As often as I look upon that treasure, and
know it to be mine, it joys me that I ever was ordained to have a being,
and to live amongst men! I must confess I am guilty of one sin, mother,
more than I brought into the world with me; but that I glory in; 'tis
theft, but noble as ever greatness yet shot up withal.
MOTHER.   How's that?
LEANTIO.   Never to be repented, mother, though sin be death! Do you now
behold her! Look on her well, she's mine; look on her better! Now, say,
if it be not the best piece of theft that ever was committed. And I have
my pardon for it. 'Tis sealed from Heaven by marriage.
MOTHER.   Married to her!
LEANTIO.   You must keep council, mother, I am undone else. If it be known,
I have lost her. From Venice her consent and I have brought her, from
parents great in wealth, more now in rage; but let storms spend their
furies. Now we have got a shelter over our quiet innocent loves, we are
contented. Little money she has brought me, view but her face, you may
see all her dowry, save that which lies locked up in hidden virtues, like
jewels kept in cabinets.
MOTHER.   You know not what you have done. What ableness have you to do her
right, in maintenance fitting her birth and virtues, which every woman of
necessity looks for, and most to go above it, not confined by their
conditions, bloods or births, but flowing to affections, wills and
humours?
LEANTIO.   Speak low, sweet mother; you are able to spoil as many as come
within the hearing. I pray do not you teach her to rebel, when she's in a
good way to obedience. I'll prove an excellent husband —here's my hand
— lay in provision, follow my business roundly, and make you a
grandmother in forty weeks! Go, pray salute her, bid her welcome
cheerfully.
MOTHER.   Gentlewoman, thus much is a debt of courtesy. [She kisses
BIANCA] And now, salute you by the name of daughter, which may challenge
more than ordinary respect. [She kisses her again]
BIANCA.   Well, this is well now, and I think few mothers of three score
will mend it.
MOTHER.   What I can bid you welcome to is mean; but make it all your own.
We are full of wants and cannot welcome worth.
LEANTIO.   Now this is scurvy! These old folks talk of nothing but defects,
because they grow so full of them themselves!
BIANCA.   Kind mother, there is nothing can be wanting to her that does
enjoy all her desires. I have forsook friends, fortunes, and my country,
and hourly I rejoice in it. I'll call this place the place of my birth
now — and rightly, too, for here my love was born, and that's the

birthday of a woman's joys. [To LEANTIO]   You have not bid me welcome
    since I came....
LEANTIO.   That I did, questionless.
BIANCA.   No sure, how was it? I have quite forgot it.
LEANTIO.   Thus. [He kisses her]
BIANCA.   Oh, sir, 'tis true, now I remember well; I have done thee wrong,
    pray take it again, sir. [She kisses him]
LEANTIO.   How many of these wrongs could I put up with in an hour? and
    turn up the glass for twice as many more!
MOTHER.   Thanks, sweet mother; the voice of her that bore me is not more
    pleasing. [They go in]
BIANCA.   Though my own care and my rich master's trust lay their commands
    both on my factorship, this day and night I'll know no other business but
    her and her dear welcome. It is a bitterness to think upon tomorrow, that
    I must leave her still to the sweet hopes of the week's end.   Oh,
    melancholy Florence! Didst thou but know what a most matchless jewel thou
    art now mistress of, a pride would take thee able to shoot destruction
    through the bonds of all thy youthful sons! But 'tis great policy to keep
    choice treasures in obscurest places;   should we show thieves our wealth
    'twould make them bolder. The jewel is cased up from all men's eyes; who
    could imagine now a gem were kept, of that great value, under this plain
    roof?   Old mothers know the world, and such as these, when sons lock
    chests, are good to look to keys.

Scene Two

GUARDIANO, FABRITIO, LIVIA.

GUARDIANO.   Has your daughter seen him yet?
FABRITIO.   No matter, she shall love him.
GUARDIANO.   Nay, let's have fair play! He has been now my ward some
    fifteen year, and it is my purpose, as time calls upon me, to tender him a
    wife. Now, sir, this wife I'd fain elect out of a daughter of yours. You
    see, my meaning's fair. If now this daughter, so tendered, should offer
    to refuse him —
FABRITIO.   I still say she shall love him.
GUARDIANO.   Yet again? And shall she have no reason for this love?
FABRITIO.   Why, do you think that women love with reason? I had a wife.
    She ran mad for me. She had no reason for it aught I could perceive.
    What do you think, lady sister? You're an experienced widow.
LIVIA.   I must offend you, then, if truth will do it, and take my niece's
    part, and call it injustice to force her love to one she never saw. Maids
    should both see and like — all little enough. If they love truly after
    that, 'tis well. She takes one man till death, that's a hard task, I tell
    you.
FABRITIO.   Why, is not man tied to the same observance, lady sister, and in
    one woman?
LIVIA.   'Tis enough for him. Besides, he tastes of many dishes that we
    poor wretches never lay our lips to — as obedience, subjection, duty and
    such kickshaws, all of our making, but served into them; and if we lick a
    finger then, sometimes, we are not to blame. Your best cooks use it.
FABRITIO.   Thou art a sweet lady, sister, and a witty.
LIVIA.   A witty! Oh, the bud of commendation, fit for a girl of sixteen!
    I am blown, man! I should be wise by this time, I have buried my two
    husbands in good fashion, and never mean more to marry.
GUARDIANO.   No, why so, lady?
LIVIA.   Because the third shall never bury me. I think I am more than
    witty. How think you, sir?
FABRITIO.   I have often paid fees to a counsellor had a weaker brain.
LIVIA.   Then I must tell you, your money was soon parted. Where is my
    niece? If you have any hope 'twill prove a wedding, 'tis fit she should
    have one sight of him.
FABRITIO.   Look out her uncle, and you are sure of her. Those two are

never asunder. They've been heard in argument at midnight, moonshine nights are noondays with them, they walk out their sleeps. They're like a chain, draw but one link, all follows.

HIPPOLITO, ISABELLA enter.

GUARDIANO.   Oh affinity, what piece of excellent workmanship art thou? It's work clean wrought, for there's no lust but love in it, and that abundantly, when in stranger things, there is no love at all but what lust brings....

FABRITIO [to ISABELLA].   On with your mask, for it's your part to see now, and not be seen. See what you mean to like — nay, and I charge you — like what you see. Do you hear me? There's no dallying. The gentleman's almost twenty, and it's time he was getting lawful heirs, and you abreeding on 'em.

ISABELLA.   Good father!

FABRITIO.   Tell me not of tongues and rumours! You'll say the gentleman is somewhat simple — the better for a husband, were you wise, for those that marry fools live ladies' lives. On with the mask, I'll hear no more. He's rich, the fool's hid under bushels.

LIVIA.   Not so hid, neither, but here's a great foul piece of him, methinks, what will he be when he comes altogether?

Enter WARD and SORDIDO, with trapsticks.

WARD.   Beat him? I beat him out the field with his own catstick, yet gave him the first hand!

SORDIDO.   Oh, strange...!

WARD.   I did it, then he set jacks on me.

SORDIDO.   What, my lady's tailor?

WARD.   Ay and I beat him, too!

SORDIDO.   Nay, that's no wonder, he's used to beating....

WARD.   I tickled him when I came once to my tippings!

SORDIDO.   Now you talk on 'em, there was a poulterer's wife made a great complaint of you last night to your guardiner, that you struck a bump in her child's head as big as an egg!

WARD.   An egg may prove a chicken, then in time the poulterer's wife will get by it. When I am in game I am furious; came my mother's eyes in my way I would not lose a fair end! No, were she alive with but one tooth in her head, I should venture the striking out of that! Coads me, my guardiner! Prithee lay up my cat and catstick safe!

GUARDIANO.   Ward!

WARD.   I feel myself after any exercise horribly prone...let me but ride, I'm lusty — a cock-horse straight, in faith!

GUARDIANO.   Ward! I must new school you!

WARD.   School me? I scorn that now, I am past schooling. I am not so base to learn to read and write, I was born to better fortunes in my cradle. [GUARDIANO, SORDIDO, WARD go out]

FABRITIO.   How do you like him, girl? This is your husband.

LIVIA.   Oh, soft there, brother! Though you be a justice, your warrant cannot be served out of your territory. You may compel, out of the power of a father, things merely harsh to a maid's flesh and blood, but when you come to love, there the soil alters.

FABRITIO.   Marry him she shall then; let her agree upon love afterwards. [He goes out. LIVIA kisses HIPPOLITO on the cheek]

LIVIA.   Prithee, cheer up thy niece with special counsel.... [She goes out]

HIPPOLITO.   I would 'twere fit to speak to her what I would, but 'twas not a thing ordained, Heaven has forbid it. Feed inward, you my sorrows, make no noise; consume me silent, let me be stark dead ere the world know I'm sick....

ISABELLA.   Marry a fool! Oh, the heartbreakings of miserable maids, where love's enforced! The best condition is but bad enough — when women have their choices, commonly they do but buy their thraldoms, and bring great

portions to men to keep 'em in subjection. Men buy their slaves, but
women buy their masters. What, are you sad too, uncle? 'Faith, then
there's a whole household down together; where shall I seek my comfort
now, when my best friend's distressed? What is it afflicts you sir?
HIPPOLITO.   'Faith, nothing but one grief that will not leave me.
ISABELLA.   Oh, be cheered, sweet uncle, how long has it been upon you? I
never spied it! How long, I pray, sir?
HIPPOLITO.   Since I first saw you, niece, and left Bologna.
ISABELLA.   And could you deal so unkindly with my heart, to keep it up so
long hid from my pity?
HIPPOLITO.   You of all creatures, niece, must never hear on it. 'Tis not a
thing ordained for you to know.
ISABELLA.   Not I, sir! All my joys that word cuts off! You made pro-
fession once you loved me best — 'twas but profession!
HIPPOLITO.   Yes, I do it truly, and fear I shall be chid for it. Know the
worst, then. I love thee dearlier than an uncle can.
ISABELLA.   Why, so you ever said, and I believed it!
HIPPOLITO.   So simple is the goodness of her thoughts they understand not
yet the unhallowed language of a sinner. I must yet be forced to come
nearer. As a man loves his wife, so I love thee.
ISABELLA.   What's that? Methought I heard ill news come towards me, which
commonly we hear too soon. It shall never come so near mine ear again.
Farewell all friendly solaces and discourses, I'll learn to live without
ye, for your dangers are greater than your comforts! [She goes out]

Scene Three

LEANTIO.

LEANTIO.   Methinks I'm even as dull now at departure as men observe great
gallants the next day after a revels; you shall see 'em look much of my
fashion, if you mark 'em well. 'Tis even a second hell to part from
pleasure when man has got a smack of it.

BIANCA and MOTHER enter, above.

I have no power to go now and I should be hanged. Farewell all business!
I desire no more than I see yonder. Let the goods at quay look to
themselves, why should I toil my youth out? Oh, fie, what a religion have
I leaped into! Get out again, for shame! The man loves best when his
care's most — that shows his zeal to love. Good to make sport when the
chest's full and the long warehouse cracks.
BIANCA.   I perceive, sir, you are not gone yet. I have good hope you'll
stay now.
LEANTIO.   Farewell, I must not.
BIANCA.   Come, come pray return. Tomorrow, adding but a little care more,
will despatch all as well — believe me, it will, sir.
LEANTIO.   I could well wish myself where you would have me; but love
that's wanton must be ruled awhile by love that's careful, or all goes to
ruin.
BIANCA.   But this one night, I prithee....
LEANTIO.   Alas, I'm in for twenty if I stay. Again, farewell to thee....
BIANCA.   Since it must, farewell, too.... [He goes out]
MOTHER.   'Faith, daughter, you are to blame. You take the course to make
him an ill husband, troth you do, and that disease is catching, I can tell
you. What cause have you to weep? Would that I had no more, that have
lived threescore years! His absence cannot last five days at utmost.

Enter applauding crowd.

BIANCA [recovering].   What's the meaning of this hurry, can you tell,
Mother?
MOTHER.   What a memory I have! I see by that years come upon me. Why

'tis a yearly custom and solemnity, religiously observed by the duke and
state to St Mark's Temple, the fifteenth of April. See if my dull brains
had not quite forgot it! I would not be ten years younger again that you
had lost the sight. Now you shall see our duke, a goodly gentleman of his
years.

BIANCA.   Is he old, then?

MOTHER.   About fifty-five.

BIANCA.   That's no great age in a man. He's then at best for wisdom and
for judgement.

MOTHER.   You shall behold all our chief states of Florence. Take this
stool.

DUKE enters, with CARDINAL and HIPPOLITO.

DUKE [to CARDINAL].   Brother, what is it commands your eye so powerfully?
Speak, you seem lost!

CARDINAL.   The thing I look on seems so. To my eyes lost forever.

DUKE.   You look on me.

CARDINAL.   What grief it is to a religious feeling to think a man should
have a friend so goodly, so wise, so noble, nay, a duke, a brother, and
all this certainly damned!

DUKE [seeing BIANCA, stops, stares up].   How?

CARDINAL.   'Tis no wonder, if your great sin can do it. Dare you sleep,
for fear of never waking but to death? And dedicate upon a strumpet's
love the strength of your affections, zeal, and health? I shall show you
how more unfortunate you stand in sin than the low private man. All his
offences, like enclosed grounds, keep but about himself and seldom stretch
his own soul's bounds, but great man, ever sin thou commit'st shows like a
flame upon a mountain, 'tis seen far about, and with a big wind made of
popular breath, the sparkles fly through cities!

DUKE [still gazing up].   If you have done, I have. No more, sweet
brother....

CARDINAL.   I know time spent in goodness is too tedious. How dare you
venture on eternal pain that cannot bear a minute's reprehension? Oh, my
brother, what were you, if you were taken now! Think upon it, brother!
Can you come so near it for a fair strumpet's love, and fall into a
torment that knows neither end nor bottom?

DUKE [tearing his eyes away, looking to CARDINAL].   Brother of spotless
honour, let me weep the first of my repentance on thy bosom, and show the
blest fruits of a thankful spirit. And if I ever keep a woman more
unlawfully, may I want penitence at my greatest need.... [The CARDINAL
smiles with joy, kisses his hand. With a parting glance at BIANCA, THE
DUKE moves on]

MOTHER.   How like you, daughter?

BIANCA.   Methinks my soul could dwell upon the reverence of such a solemn
and most worthy custom. Did not the duke look up? Methought he saw us.

MOTHER.   That's everyone's conceit that sees a duke!

BIANCA.   Most likely so.

MOTHER.   Come, come, we'll end this argument below!

Scene Four

HIPPOLITO, LIVIA.

LIVIA.   A strange affection, brother, when I think on't! I wonder how thou
camest by it.

HIPPOLITO.   Even as easily as man comes by destruction, which oft-times he
wears in his own bosom.

LIVIA.   Is the world so populous in women, and creation so prodigal in
beauty and so various, yet does love turn thy point to thine own blood?
'Tis somewhat too unkindly. Must thy eye dwell evilly on the fairness of
thy kindred, and seek not where it should?

HIPPOLITO.   Never was man's misery so soon sewed up.

LIVIA. Nay, I love you so, that I shall venture much to keep a change from you so fearful as this grief will bring upon you. Let not passion waste the goodness of thy time and of thy fortune. I can bring forth as pleasant fruits as sensuality wishes in all her teeming longings. This I can do.

HIPPOLITO. Oh, nothing that can make my wishes perfect....

LIVIA. Sir, I could give as shrewd a lift to chastity as any she that wears a tongue in Florence. She'd need to be a good horsewoman and sit fast whom my strong argument could not fling at last.

HIPPOLITO. I am past hope.

LIVIA. You are not the first, brother, has attempted things more forbidden than this seems to be. Thou shalt see me do a strange cure as ever was wrought on a disease so mortal and near akin to shame. When shall you see her?

HIPPOLITO. Never in comfort more.

LIVIA. You're so impatient, too.

HIPPOLITO. Will you believe — 'death, she has forsworn my company, and sealed it with a blush.

LIVIA. So, I perceive, all lies upon my hands, then. The more glory when the work's finished. [She kisses him] Your absence, gentle brother. I must bestir my wits for you.

HIPPOLITO. Ay, to great purpose. [He goes out]

LIVIA. I take a course to pity him so much now, that I have none left for modesty and myself. This 'tis to grow so liberal — you have few sisters that love their brother's ease above their own honesties. [Enter ISABELLA] Niece, your love's welcome. Alas, what draws that paleness to thy cheeks? This enforced marriage?

ISABELLA. It helps, good aunt, amongst some other griefs.

LIVIA. Indeed, the ward is simple.

ISABELLA. Simple! That were well! Why, one might make good shift with such a husband. But he's a fool entailed, he halts downright in it.

LIVIA. And knowing this, I hope 'tis at your choice to take or refuse, niece.

ISABELLA. You see it is not. I loathe him more than beauty can hate death.

LIVIA. Let it appear, then.

ISABELLA. How can I, being born with that obedience that must submit unto a father's will?

LIVIA. Be not offended, prithee, if I set by the name of niece awhile, and bring in pity in a stranger fashion. It lies here in this breast, would cross this match.

ISABELLA. How, cross it, aunt?

LIVIA. Ay, and give thee more liberty than thou hast reason yet to apprehend.

ISABELLA. Sweet aunt, in goodness keep not hid from me what may befriend my life.

LIVIA. Yes, yes, I must when I return to reputation, and think upon the solemn vow I made to your dead mother, my most loving sister...'twas a secret I have took special care of, delivered by your mother on her deathbed — that's nine years now, and I'll not part from it yet, though never was fitter time nor greater cause for it!

ISABELLA. As you desire the praises of a virgin!

LIVIA. Good sorrow! I would do thee any kindness! [Pause, she seems to suffer] Let it suffice, you may refuse this fool, or you may take him as you see occasion. You cannot be enforced.

ISABELLA. Sweet aunt, deal plainer.

LIVIA. Say I should trust you now upon an oath, and give you in a secret that would start you. How am I sure of you, in faith and silence?

ISABELLA. Equal assurance may I find in mercy, as you for that in me.

LIVIA. It shall suffice. Then know, however custom has made good, for reputation's sake, the names of niece and aunt 'twixt you and I, we are nothing less.

ISABELLA. How's that?

LIVIA. I told you I should start your blood. You are no more allied to

any of us than the merest stranger is, or one begot at Naples when the husband lies at Rome. Did never the report of that famed Spaniard, Marquess of Coria, since your time was ripe for understanding, fill your ear with wonder?
ISABELLA.   Yes, what of him?   I have heard his deeds of honour often related when we lived in Naples.
LIVIA.   You heard the praises of your father, then.
ISABELLA.   My father!
LIVIA.   That was he.   But all the business so carefully and so discreetly carried that fame received no spot by it, not a blemish.   How weak his commands now, whom you call father?   How vain all his enforcements, your obedience?   And what a largeness in your will and liberty to take or reject, or to do both?   For fools will serve to father wise men's children — all this you have time to think on.   Oh, my wench, nothing overthrows our sex but indiscretion!   But keep your thoughts to yourself, from all the world, kindred or dearest friend — nay, I entreat you, from him that all this while you have called uncle;   and though you love him dearly, as I know his deserts claim as much even from a stranger, yet let not him know this, I prithee do not.
ISABELLA.   Believe my oath, I will not.
LIVIA.   Why, well said.... [She turns to go]   Who shows more craft to undo a maidenhead, I'll resign my part to her.   [HIPPOLITO comes in] She's thine own, go.   [LIVIA goes out]
ISABELLA.   Have I passed so much time in ignorance, and never had the means to know myself till this blest hour!   Thanks to her virtuous pity that brought it now to light — would I had known it but one day sooner, he had then received in favours what, poor gentleman, he took in bitter words!   [She turns to him]   Prithee, forgive me.   I did but chide in jest;   the best loves use it sometimes, it sets and edge upon affection. When we invite our best friends to a feast, 'tis not all sweetmeats that we set before them, there's somewhat sharp and salt both to whet the appetite and make 'em taste their wine well.   So, methinks, after a friendly, sharp and savoury chiding, a kiss tastes wondrous well and full of the grape — [She kisses him]   How thinks't thou, does't not?
HIPPOLITO.   'Tis so excellent, I know not how to praise it, what to say to it!
ISABELLA.   The marriage shall go forward.
HIPPOLITO.   With the ward? Are you in earnest?
ISABELLA.   Should my father provide a worse fool yet I'ld have him either. The worse the better.   So discretion love me, desert and judgement, I have content sufficient.   Pray make your love no stranger, sir, that's all. [She goes out]
HIPPOLITO.   Never came joys so unexpectedly to meet desires in man.   How came she thus?   But I'm thankful for it.   This marriage now must of necessity go forward, it is the only veil wit can devise to keep our acts hid from sin-piercing eyes.

Scene Five

GUARDIANO and LIVIA.

LIVIA.   How, sir, a gentlewoman so young, so fair, as you set forth, spied from the widow's window?
GUARDIANO.   She!
LIVIA.   Our Sunday-dinner woman?
GUARDIANO.   And Thursday-supper woman, the same still.   I know not how she came by her, but I'll swear she's the prime gallant for a face in Florence, and no doubt other parts follow their leader.   The duke himself first spied her at the window, then in a rapture, as if admiration were poor when it were single, beckoned me, and pointed to the wonder warily. I never knew him so infinitely taken with a woman, nor can I blame his appetite, she's a creature able to draw a state from serious business. What course shall we devise? He has spoken twice now.

LIVIA.   Twice?   I long myself to see this absolute creature that wins the
heart of love and praise so much.
GUARDIANO.   Shall you entreat her company? I would 'twere done, the duke
waits the good hour, and I wait the good fortune that may spring from it.
[FABRITIO comes in]   Signor Fabritio!
FABRITIO.   Oh, sir, I bring an alteration in my mouth now! My daughter
loves him.
GUARDIANO.   What, does she, sir?
FABRITIO.   No talk but of the ward, she would have him to choose 'bove all
men she ever saw.
GUARDIANO.   Why, then, sir, if you'll have me speak my thoughts, I smell
'twill be a match.
FABRITIO.   Ay, and a sweet young couple if I have any judgement.
GUARDIANO.   Let her be sent tomorrow before noon, and handsomely tricked
up.
FABRITIO.   I warrant you for handsome. I will see her things laid ready,
every one in order, and have some part of her tricked up tonight. 'Twas a
use her mother had when invited to an early wedding; she'ld dress her
head o'ernight, sponge up herself, and give her neck three lathers.
GUARDIANO.   Ne'er a halter?
FABRITIO.   On with her chain of pearl, her ruby bracelets, lay ready all
her tricks and jiggambobs.
GUARDIANO.   So must your daughter.   [FABRITIO goes out]
LIVIA.   How he sweats in the foolish zeal of fatherhood...and here comes
his sweet son-in-law that shall be. They're both allied in wit before the
marriage, what will they be hereafter, when they are nearer?

She goes out.   THE WARD and SORDIDO enter, with shuttlecocks and
battledores.

GUARDIANO.   Now, young heir!
WARD.   What's the next business after shuttlecock?
GUARDIANO.   Tomorrow you shall see the gentlewoman must be your wife.
WARD.   There's even another thing too must be kept up with a pair of
battledores. My wife! What can she do?
GUARDIANO.   Nay, that's a question you should ask yourself, ward, when
you're alone together.
WARD.   That's as I list! A wife's to be asked anywhere, I hope. I'll ask
her in a congregation, if I have a mind to it, and so save a licence.
SORDIDO.   Let me be at the choosing of your beloved, if you desire a woman
of good parts.
WARD.   Thou shalt, sweet Sordido!
SORDIDO.   I have a plaguey guess. Let me alone to see what she is. If I
but look upon her — 'way, I know all the faults to a hair you may refuse
her for.
WARD.   Dost thou? I prithee let me hear 'em, Sordido.
SORDIDO.   Well, mark 'em then. I have 'em all in rhyme.

    The wife your guardiner ought to tender
    Should be pretty, straight and slender;
    Her hair not short, her foot not long,
    Her hand not huge, nor too loud her tongue;
    No pearl in eye nor ruby in her nose,
    No burn or cut but what the catalogue shows.
    She must have teeth, and that no black ones,
    And kiss most sweet when she does smack once;
    Her skin must be both white and plumpt,
    Her body straight, not hopper rumped,
    Or wriggle sideways like a crab.
    She must be neither slut nor drab,
    Nor go too splay-foot with her shoes
    To make her smock lick up the dews.
    And two things more which I forgot to tell ye;
    She neither must have bump in back nor belly.

These are the faults which will not make her pass.

WARD.   And if I spy not these I am a rank ass!

SORDIDO.   You should see her naked, for that's the ancient order.

WARD.   See her naked? That were good sport, in faith, but stay! How if she should desire to see me so too? I were in a sweet case, then; such a foul skin!

SORDIDO.   But you have a clean shirt, sir, and that makes amends.

WARD.   'Faith, choosing of a wench in a huge farthingale is like buying of ware under a great penthouse; what with the deceit of one, and the false light of the other, mark my speeches, he may have a diseased wench in his bed, and rotten stuff in his breeches! [They whoop with laughter, go out]

LIVIA [entering with THE MOTHER].   Widow, come, come! I have a great quarrel to you, 'faith, I must chide you, that you must be sent for! You cannot be more welcome to any house in Florence!

MOTHER.   My thanks must needs acknowledge so much, madam.

LIVIA.   I sit here sometimes whole days without company! I know you are alone, too, why should we not we, like two kind neighbours, then, supply the wants of one another, having tongue-discourse, experience in the world, and such kind helps to laugh down time, and meet age merrily?

MOTHER.   Age, madam! You speak mirth. 'Tis at my door, but a long journey from your ladyship yet.

LIVIA.   My faith, I'm nine and thirty, every stroke, wench, and 'tis a general observation, wives or widows, we account ourselves then old, when young men's eyes leave looking at us. Come, now, I have thy company I'll not part with it till after supper.

MOTHER.   Yes, I must crave pardon, madam —

LIVIA.   I swear you shall stay supper.

MOTHER.   Some other time I will make bold —

GUARDIANO.   Nay, pray stay, widow.

LIVIA.   Faith, she shall not go. Do you think I'll be forsworn? [She brings table and chess]

MOTHER.   'Tis a great while till supper time. I'll take my leave then now, madam, and come again in the evening —

LIVIA.   In the evening! By my troth, wench, you have great business, sure, to sit alone at home! I wonder strangely what pleasure you take in it! Come, we'll to chess or draughts; there are an hundred tricks to drive out time till supper, never fear.

MOTHER.   I'll make but one step home and return straight, madam.

LIVIA.   I'll not trust you, you use more excuses to your kind friends than ever I knew any! What business can you have, if you be sure you have locked the door?

MOTHER.   As good as tell her now, then, for she will know it. I have always found her a most friendly lady. [She turns to LIVIA] To tell you truth, I left a gentlewoman even sitting all alone, which is uncomfortable, especially to young bloods.

LIVIA.   What gentlewoman? Pish! Another excuse!

MOTHER.   Wife to my son indeed, but not known, madam, to any but yourself.

LIVIA.   Now I beshrew you! Could you be so unkind to her and me, to come and not bring her?

MOTHER.   I feared to be too bold. And she's a stranger, madam.

LIVIA.   The more should be her welcome. Make some amends, and fetch her, go.

MOTHER [rising to go].   It must be carried wondrous privately from my son's knowledge; he'll break out in storms else. [She goes out]

LIVIA.   Now comes in the heat of your part.

GUARDIANO.   True, I know it, lady, and if I be out, may the duke banish me from all employments, wanton or serious. [BIANCA comes in, curtsies]

LIVIA.   Gentlewoman, you are most welcome, trust me, you are, as courtesy can make one, or respect due to the presence of you.

BIANCA.   I give you thanks, lady.

LIVIA.   I heard you were alone, and it had appeared an ill condition in me to have kept your company here from you and left you all solitary. [To MOTHER] Come widow — look you, lady, here's our business. Are we not well employed, think you? An old quarrel between us, that will never be at an end. I pray, sit down forsooth, if you have the patience to look upon two weak and tedious gamesters....

GUARDIANO.   'Faith, madam, set these by till evening. The gentlewoman, being a stranger, would take more delight to see your rooms and pictures.

LIVIA.   Marry, good sir, and well remembered! I beseech you show 'em her, that will beguile time well. Here, take these keys, show her the monument too — and that's a thing everyone sees not, you can witness that, widow!

MOTHER.   And that's a worth sight indeed, madam.

BIANCA.   Kind lady, I fear I came to be a trouble to you, and to this courteous gentleman that wears a kindness in his breast so noble and bounteous.

GUARDIANO.   If you but give acceptance to my service, you do the greatest grace and honour to me that courtesy can merit.

BIANCA.   I pray you lead, sir.

LIVIA.   After a game or two, we are for you, gentlefolks.... [They go out. LIVIA plays chess] Alas, poor widow, I shall be too hard for thee.

MOTHER.   You're cunning at the game, I'll be sworn, madam....

LIVIA.   It will be found so, ere I give you over.... She that can place her man well....

MOTHER.   As you do, madam....

LIVIA.   As I shall, wench, can never lose her game. Nay, nay, the black king's mine.

MOTHER.   Cry you mercy, madam.

LIVIA.   And this my queen.

MOTHER.   I see it now.

LIVIA.   Here's a duke will strike a sure stroke for the game anon; your pawn cannot come back to relieve itself.

MOTHER.   I know that, madam.

LIVIA.   You play well the whilst. How she belies her skill. I give you check and mate to your white king, simplicity itself.

MOTHER.   Well, ere now, lady, I have seen the fall of subtlety. Jest on! What remedy but patience! [GUARDIANO and BIANCA, above]

BIANCA.   Trust me, sir, mine eye never met with fairer ornaments.

GUARDIANO.   Nay, livelier, I'm persuaded, neither Florence nor Venice can produce.

BIANCA.   Sir, my opinion takes your part highly.

GUARDIANO.   There's a better piece yet, than all these.... [Enter unseen the DUKE]

BIANCA.   Not possible, sir!

GUARDIANO.   Believe it. You'll say so when you see it. Turn but your eye now. [He goes out]

BIANCA.   Oh, sir!

DUKE.   He's gone, beauty! Pish, not look after him, he's but a vapour that when the sun appears is seen no more.

BIANCA.   Oh, treachery to honour!

DUKE.   Prithee, tremble not. I feel thy breast shake like a turtle panting under a loving hand that makes much on't. Why art so fearful? As I'm friend to brightness, there's nothing but respect and honour near thee. You know me, you have seen me; here's a heart can witness I've seen thee.

BIANCA.   The more's my danger.

DUKE.   The more's thy happiness. Pish, strive not, sweet! This strength were excellent employed in love, now, but here 'tis spent amiss. Strive not to seek thy liberty and keep me still in prison.

BIANCA.   Oh, my lord!

DUKE.   Take warning, I beseech thee. Thou seem'st to me a creature so composed of gentleness I should be sorry the least force should lay an unkind touch upon thee.

BIANCA.   Oh, my extremity! My lord, what seek you?

DUKE.   Love.

BIANCA.   'Tis gone already, I have a husband.

DUKE.   That's a single comfort. Take a friend to him.

BIANCA.   That's a double mischief, or else there's no religion.

DUKE.   Do not tremble at fears of thine own making.

BIANCA.   Nor great lord, make me not bold with death and deeds of ruin because they fear not you.

DUKE.   Sure, I think thou know'st the way to please me. I affect a
passionate pleading above an easy yielding — but never pitied any. They
deserve none that will not pity me. I can command. Think upon that.

BIANCA.   Why should you seek, sir, to take away that you can never give?

DUKE.   But I give better in exchange! Wealth, honour! She that is
fortunate in a duke's favour lights on a tree that bears all women's
wishes. If your own mother saw you pluck fruit there, she would commend
your wit and praise the time of your nativity. Take hold of glory. Do
not I know you have cast away your life upon necessities, means merely
doubtful to keep you in indifferent health and fashion — a thing I heard
too lately and soon pitied...? And can you be so much your beauty's enemy
to kiss away a month or two in wedlock, and weep whole years in wants for
ever after? Come, play the wise wench and provide for ever.... [They go
out]

LIVIA.   Did I not say my duke would fetch you over, widow?

MOTHER.   I think you spoke in earnest when you said it, madam....

LIVIA.   And my black king makes all the haste he can, too, I have given
thee blind mate twice...!

MOTHER.   You may see, madam, my eyes begin to fail....

LIVIA.   I'll swear they do....

GUARDIANO [entering].   I can but smile as often as I think on it! How
prettily the poor fool was beguiled, how unexpectedly! It is a witty age,
never were finer snares for women's honesties than are devised in these
days. Yet to prepare her stomach by degrees to Cupid's feast, I showed
her naked pictures by the way — a bit to stay the appetite....

LIVIA.   The game's even at the best now. You may see widow, how all things
draw to an end. Has not my duke bestirred himself?

MOTHER.   Yes, 'faith, madam, he has done me all the mischief in this
game....

BIANCA [entering].   Now bless me from a blasting! I saw that now fearful
for any woman's eye to look on. Infectious mists and mildews hang at his
eyes, the weather of a doomsday dwells upon him. Yet, since mine honour's
leprous, why should I preserve that fair that caused the leprosy? Come
poison all at once! Thou in whose baseness the bane of virtue broods, I'm
bound in soul eternally to curse thy smooth-browed treachery that wore the
fair veil of a friendly welcome! And I a stranger, think upon it!
Murders piled up upon a guilty spirit at his last breath will not lie
heavier than this betraying act upon thy conscience. I'm made bold now, I
thank thy treachery. Sin and I'm acquainted, no couple greater.

GUARDIANO.   Well, so the duke loves me I fare not much amiss, then. Two
great feasts do seldom come together in one day.

BIANCA.   What, still at it, mother?

MOTHER.   You see we sit by it. Are you so soon returned? You have not
seen all, since, surely?

BIANCA.   That have I, Mother, the monument and all! 'Faith, I have seen
that I little thought to see in the morning when I rose....

MOTHER.   Nay, so I told you before you saw it, it would prove worth your
sight.   I give you great thanks for my daughter, sir, and all your
kindness towards her.

GUARDIANO.   Oh, good widow! Much good may it do her — forty weeks hence,
in faith...!

LIVIA [rising].   We'll walk to supper. [To BIANCA] Will it please you,
gentlewoman?

BIANCA.   Thanks, virtuous lady — you are a damned bawd! I'll follow you,
forsooth. Pray take my mother in, this gentleman and I vow not to part...
[She and GUARDIANO go out. MOTHER leads the way]

LIVIA.   Are you so bitter? 'Tis but want of use, her tender modesty is
sea-sick a little, being not accustomed to the breaking billow of woman's
wavering faith, blown with temptations. Sin tastes at the first draught
like wormwood bitter, but drunk again, 'tis nectar ever after.

Scene Six

THE MOTHER.

MOTHER. I would my son would either keep at home or I were in my grave! She was but one day abroad but ever since she's grown so cutted, there's no speaking to her. Whether the sight of great cheer at my lady's, and such mean fare at home, work discontent in her, I know not, but I'm sure she's strangely altered. I'll never keep daughter-in-law in the house with me again if I had a hundred.

BIANCA [entering]. This is the strangest house for all defects as ever gentlewoman made shift withal to pass away her love in! Why is there not a cushion cloth of drawn work, or some fair cut-work pinned up in my bedchamber, a silver and gilt casting bottle hung by it?

MOTHER. She talks of things here my whole state's not worth....

BIANCA. Never a green silk quilt is there in the house, mother, to cast upon my bed?

MOTHER. No, by troth is there! Nor orange-tawny, neither.

BIANCA. Here's a house for a young gentlewoman to be got with child in!

MOTHER. What, cannot children be begot, think you, without gilt casting-bottles? 'Tis an old saying, 'one may keep good cheer in a mean house'.

BIANCA. Troth, you speak wondrous well for your old house here, 'twill shortly fall down at your feet to thank you. Must I live in want because my fortune matched me with your son? I ask less now than what I had at home when I was a maid, kept short of that which a wife knows she must have, nay, and will! Will, mother, if she be not a fool born. And report went of me that I could wrangle for what I wanted when I was two hours old...! [She goes out]

MOTHER. When she first lighted here, I told her then how mean she should find all things — she was pleased forsooth! None better! I laid open all defects to her, she was contented still! But the devil's in her. What course shall I think on? She frets me so....

LEANTIO [entering]. How near I am now to happiness that earth exceeds not. Not another like it! I scent the air of blessings when I come but near the house! Honest wedlock is like a banqueting house built in a garden, when base lust with all her powders, paintings and best pride is but a fair house built by a ditch side. Now for a welcome able to draw men's envies upon man! After a five days' fast she'll be so greedy now, and cling about me, I take care how I shall be rid of her! And here it begins! [BIANCA and MOTHER enter]

BIANCA. Oh, sir, you are welcome home.

LEANTIO. Is that all? Why this? Sure you are not well, Bianca. How dost, prithee?

BIANCA. I have been better than I am.

LEANTIO. Alas, I thought so.

BIANCA. Nay, I have been worse, too, that now you see me, sir.

LEANTIO. I'm glad thou mend'st yet. I feel my heart mend, too. How came it to thee? Has anything disliked thee in my absence?

BIANCA. No, certain...I have had the best content that Florence can afford....

LEANTIO. Thou mak'st the best of it. Speak, mother, what's the cause? You must needs know.

MOTHER. Troth, I know none, son. Let her speak herself.

BIANCA. Methinks this house stands nothing to my mind, I'ld have some pleasant lodging in the high street, sir. Or if it were near the court, that were much better — 'tis a sweet recreation for a gentlewoman to stand in a bay window and see gallants.

LEANTIO. Now, I have another temper, a mere stranger to that of yours, it seems. I should delight to see none but yourself.

BIANCA. I praise not that. Too fond is as unseemly as too churlish. I would not have a husband of that proneness to kiss me before company, for a world! Beside, 'tis tedious to see one thing still, sir, be it the best that ever heart affected. You are learned, sir, and know I speak not

ill. 'Tis full as virtuous for a woman's eye to look on several men as
for her heart, sir, to be fixed on one....

LEANTIO.   Now thou com'st home to me! A kiss for that word!

BIANCA.   No matter for a kiss, sir, let it pass. Let's talk of other
business and forget it. What news now of the pirates? Any stirring?

MOTHER.   I'm glad he's here yet to see her tricks himself. I had lied
monstrously if I had told 'em first.

LEANTIO.   Speak, what's the humour, sweet, you make your lip so strange?
This was not wont.

BIANCA.   Is there no kindness betwixt man and wife unless they make a
pigeon-house of friendship and be still billing? Alas, sir, think of the
world, how we shall live, grow serious. We have been married a whole
fortnight now.

LEANTIO.   How, a whole fortnight! Is that long? [A knock] Who's there,
now? Withdraw you, Bianca, thou art a gem no stranger's eye must see,
however thou please now to look dull on me. [She goes out. A MESSENGER
enters] You're welcome, sir. To whom your business, pray?

MESSENGER.   To one I see not here, now.

LEANTIO.   Who should that be?

MESSENGER.   A young gentlewoman I was sent to.

LEANTIO.   A young gentlewoman?

MESSENGER.   Ay, sir, about sixteen. Why look you so wildly?

LEANTIO.   At your strange error. You have mistook the house, there's none
such here, I assure you.

MESSENGER.   I assure you, too. The man that sent me cannot be mistook.

LEANTIO.   Why, who is it sent you, sir?

MESSENGER.   The duke.

LEANTIO.   The duke! Troth, shall I tell you, sir, it is the most erroneous
business that e'er your honest pains were abused with. His grace has been
most wondrous ill-informed. Pray so return it, sir. What should her name
be?

MESSENGER.   Then I shall tell you straight, too. Bianca Capello.

LEANTIO.   How, sir, Bianca? What do you call the other?

MESSENGER.   Capello. Sir, it seems you know no such, then?

LEANTIO.   I never heard of the name.

MESSENGER.   Then 'tis a sure mistake. I will return and seek no further.
[He goes]

LEANTIO.   Come forth, Bianca. Thou art betrayed, I fear me.

BIANCA [appearing].   Betrayed? How, sir?

LEANTIO.   The duke knows thee.

BIANCA.   How should the duke know me? Can you guess, mother?

MOTHER.   Not I with all my wits. Sure, we kept house close.

LEANTIO.   Kept close! Not all the locks in Italy can keep you women so!
You have been gadding, and ventured out a twilight to the court-green
yonder, without your masks. I'll be hanged else! Thou hast been seen,
Bianca, by some stranger. Never excuse it.

BIANCA.   I'll not seek the way, sir. Do you think you have married me to
mew me up not to be seen? What would you make of me?

LEANTIO.   A good wife, nothing else.

BIANCA.   Why, so are some that are seen every day, else the devil take 'em.

LEANTIO.   No more, then. I believe all virtuous in thee without an
argument. 'Twas but thy hard chance to be seen somewhere....

MOTHER.   Now I can tell you son, the time and place!

LEANTIO.   When? Where?

MOTHER.   What wits have I! When you last took your leave, if you remember,
you left us both at window. And not the third part of an hour after the
duke passed by in great solemnity. He looked up twice to the window.

LEANTIO.   Looked he up twice! And could you take no warning?

MOTHER.   Why, once may do as much harm, son, as a thousand, do you not know
one spark has fired an house as well as a whole furnace?

LEANTIO.   My heart flames for it! Yet let's be wise and keep all smothered
closely. I have bethought a means. Is the door fast?

MOTHER.   I locked it myself after him.

LEANTIO.   You know, mother, at the end of the dark parlour there's a place

so artificially contrived no search could ever find it.   There will I lock
my life's best treasure up. Bianca!

BIANCA.   Would you keep me closer yet? Have you the conscience?

LEANTIO.   Why, are you so insensible of your danger to ask that now? The
duke himself has sent for you!

BIANCA.   Has he so! And you the man would never yet vouchsafe to tell me
of it till now.   You show your loyalty and honesty at once, and so,
farewell, sir.

LEANTIO.   Bianca, whither now?

BIANCA.   Why, to the duke, sir, you say he sent for me.

LEANTIO.   But thou dost not mean to go, I hope?

BIANCA.   No? I shall prove unmannerly, rude and uncivil, mad, and imitate
you?   Come, mother, come, follow his humour no longer.   We shall all be
executed for treason shortly.

MOTHER.   Not I, in faith.   I'll first obey the duke, and taste of a good
banquet. I'm of thy mind.

BIANCA.   Why, here's an old wench would trot into a bawd now for a piece of
fruit or marzipan! [They go out]

LEANTIO.   Oh, thou the ripe time of man's misery, wedlock, when all his
thoughts, like over-laden trees, crack with the fruits they bear, in cares
and jealousies.   What a peace has he that never marries! If he knew the
benefit he enjoyed, or had the fortune to come and speak with me, he
should know then the infinite wealth he had, and discern rightly the
greatness of his treasure by my loss.   Nay, what a quietness he has above
mine, that wears his youth out in a strumpet's arms and never spends more
care upon a woman than at the time of lust, but walks away, and if he
finds her dead at his return, his pity is soon done.   But all the fears,
shames, jealousies, costs and troubles, and still renewed cares of a
marriage bed live in the issue when the wife is dead....

MESSENGER [entering].   Though you were pleased just now to pin an error
on me, you must not shift another in your stead too.   The duke has sent
for you.

LEANTIO.   How, for me? I see then, 'tis my theft.   Well, I'm not the first
has stolen away a maid! [They hurry out]

Scene Seven

A Banquet

GUARDIANO.   Take you especial note of such a gentlewoman, she's here on
purpose. I have invited her, her father and her uncle to this banquet.

WARD.   'Faith, I should know her now, among a thousand women.   A little,
pretty, deft and tidy thing, you say?

GUARDIANO.   Right.

WARD.   With a lusty, sprouting sprig in her hair?

GUARDIANO.   Thou goest the right way still. Take one mark more. Thou
shalt never find her hand out of her uncle's.   The love of kindred never
yet stuck closer than theirs to one another.   He that weds her marries her
uncle's heart, too.

WARD.   Say you so, sir! Then I'll be asked in the church to both of 'em!

GUARDIANO.   Fall back, here comes the duke!

WARD.   He brings a gentlewoman, I should fall forward, rather!

DUKE.   Come Bianca, of purpose sent into the world to show perfection once
in woman.   I'll believe henceforward they have every one a soul, too,
against all the uncourteous opinions that man's uncivil rudeness ever held
of 'em.   Glory of Florence, light into mine arms.

LEANTIO enters

BIANCA.   Yon comes a grudging man will chide you, sir.   The storm is now in
his heart, and would get nearer and fall here if it durst — it pours
down yonder.

DUKE.   If that be he, the weather shall soon clear.   Listen, and I'll tell thee how. [Whispers to her]

LEANTIO.   A kissing, too? I see 'tis plain lust now, adultery boldened.
What will it prove anon, when 'tis stuffed full of wine and sweetmeats,
being so impudent fasting?

DUKE.   We have heard of your good parts, sir, which we honour with our
embrace and love. Is not the captainship of Rouens' citadel, since the
late deceased, supplied by any yet?

GUARDIANO. By none, my lord.

DUKE.   Take it, the place is yours, then. [LEANTIO kneels]   And as
faithfulness and desert grows, our favour shall grow with it. Rise now,
the captain of our fort at Rouens!

LEANTIO.   The service of whole life give your grace thanks. [Aside]
This is some good yet, and more than ever I looked for — a fine bit to
stay a cuckold's stomach! All preferment that springs from sin and lust,
it shoots up quickly, as gardeners' crops do in the rottenest grounds.

LIVIA.   Is that your son, widow?

MOTHER.   Yes, did your ladyship never know that till now?

LIVIA.   No, trust me, did I. Nor ever truly felt the power of love and
pity to a man, till now I knew him. I have enough to buy me my desires,
and yet to spare, that's one good comfort. Hark you? Pray let me speak
with you, sir, before you go....

DUKE.   Here's a health now, gallants, to the best beauty at this day in
Florence!

BIANCA.   Whoe'r she be, she shall not go unpledged, sir....

DUKE.   Here's to thy health, Bianca....

BIANCA.   Nothing comes more welcome to that name than your grace....

LEANTIO.   So, so! Here stands the poor thief now that stole the treasure,
and he's not thought on.

DUKE.   Methinks there is no spirit amongst us, gallants, but what divinely
sparkles from the eyes of bright Bianca — we sat all in darkness but for
that splendour. Who was it told us lately of a match-making rite, a
marriage-tender?

GUARDIANO. 'Twas I, my lord.

DUKE.   'Twas you indeed. Where is she?

GUARDIANO. This is the gentlewoman.

FABRITIO. My lord, my daughter.

WARD.   The ape's so little, I shall scarce feel her. I have seen almost as
tall as she sold in the fair for tenpence....

FABRITIO.   She has the full qualities of a gentlewoman, I have brought her
up to music, dancing and whatnot, that may commend her sex and stir her
husband.

WARD.   See how she simpers — as if marmalade would not melt in her
mouth....

DUKE.   And which is he?

GUARDIANO. This young heir, my lord.

DUKE.   What is he brought up to?

WARD.   To cat and trap.

GUARDIANO. My lord, he's a great ward, wealthy but simple. His parts
consist in acres.

DUKE.   Oh, wise acres!

GUARDIANO. Y'have spoke him in a word, sir!

BIANCA.   'Las, poor gentlewoman, she's ill bestead, unless she's dealt the
wiselier and laid in more provision for her youth. Fools will not keep in
summer.

LEANTIO.   No, nor such wives from whores in winter.

DUKE [To FABRITIO]   Yea, the voice too, sir?

FABRITIO.   Ay, and a sweet breast too, my lord, I hope, or I have cast away
my money wisely — she took her pricksong earlier, my lord, that any of
her kindred ever did.

DUKE.   Let's turn to a better banquet, then. For music bids the soul of
man to feast! [Music]

LEANTIO.   True, and damnation has taught you that wisdom. You can take
gifts, too! Oh, that music mocks me!

LIVIA.   I am as dumb to any language now but love's, as one that never

learned to speak! I am not yet so old, but he may think of me. My own
fault — I have been idle a long time.   •

ISABELLA [singing].   What harder chance can fall to woman,
    Who was born to cleave to some man,
    Than to bestow her time, youth, beauty,
    Life's observance, honour, duty,
    On a thing for no use good
    But to make physic work, or blood
    Force fresh in an old lady's cheek?
    So that would be
    Mother of fools, let her compound with me....

WARD.   Here's a tune indeed! Pish! I would rather hear one ballad sung in
the nose now, of the lamentable drowning of fat sheep and oxen, than all
these simpering tunes played upon cat-guts and sung by little kitlings.

FABRITIO [to GUARDIANO].   Will it please you now, sir, to entreat
your ward to take her by the hand and lead her in a dance before the duke?

WARD.   Dance with her! Not I, sweet guardiner, do not urge my heart to it,
'tis clean against my blood. Dance with a stranger!

GUARDIANO.   Why, who shall take her, then?

WARD.   Look, there's her uncle! Perhaps he knows the manner of her
dancing, too?

GUARDIANO.   Thou'lt be an ass, still.

WARD.   Ay. All that 'uncle' shall not fool me out....

GUARDIANO [to HIPPOLITO].   I must entreat you, sir, to take your niece
and dance with her. My ward's a little wilful, he would have you show him
the way.

HIPPOLITO.   Me, sir! He shall command it at all hours, pray tell him so.

GUARDIANO.   I thank you for him. He has not wit himself, sir.

The Dance. Enter, surreptitiously, SORDIDO.

[To WARD] Do it when I bid you, sir....

WARD.   I'll venture but a hornpipe with her, guardiner, of some such
married man's dance....

GUARDIANO.   Well, venture something sir! [Turns. SORDIDO comes to THE
WARD's side]

WARD.   Here she's come again. Mark her now, Sordido... [He declares half
publicly] Plain men dance the measures, the cinquepence the gay;
    Cuckolds dance the hornpipe, and farmers dance the hay;
    Your soldiers dance the round, and maidens that grow big
    Your drunkards the canaries, your whore and bawd, the jig.
    Here's your eight kind of dancers — he that find the ninth,
    Let him pay the minstrels. [He goes to dance]

DUKE.   Oh, here he appears once in his own person! I thought he would
have married her by attorney, and lain with her so, too.   [THE WARD
ridiculously imitates HIPPOLITO]

BIANCA.   Methinks, if he would take some voyage when he's married,
dangerous or long enough, and scarce be seen once in nine year together, a
wife then might make indifferent shift to be content with him....

THE WARD and ISABELLA dance.

ISABELLA.   And how do you like me, now, sir?

WARD.   'Faith, so well I never mean to part with thee, sweetheart, under
some sixteen children.

GUARDIANO.   How now, ward and nephew, speak, is it so, or not?

WARD.   'Tis so, we are both agreed, sir. [GUARDIANO bows to THE DUKE]

DUKE.   My thanks to all your loves! Come, fair Bianca, we have took
special care of you, and provided your lodging near us now.

BIANCA.   Your love is great, my lord.

DUKE.   Once more, our thanks to all.

ALL.   All blest honours guard you!

LEANTIO.   Oh, hast thou left me then, Bianca, utterly! Bianca, now I miss
thee — oh, return, and save the faith of woman. I never felt the loss

of thee till now, 'tis an affliction of greater weight than youth was made to bear!

LIVIA.   Sweet sir!

LEANTIO.   As long as mine eye saw thee, I half enjoyed thee....

LIVIA.   Sir?

LEANTIO.   Canst thou forget the dear pains my love took, how it has watched whole nights together in all weathers for thee, yet stood in heart more merry than the tempests that sung about mine ears, and then received thee from thy father's window into these arms at midnight, when we embraced as if we had been statues only made for it, to show art's life, so silent were our comforts....

LIVIA.   This makes me madder to enjoy him now. Sir!

LEANTIO.   Cry mercy, lady! What would you say to me? My sorrow makes me so unmannerly, I had quite forgot you.

LIVIA.   Nothing, but even in pity to that passion, would give your grief good counsel.

LEANTIO.   Marry, and welcome, lady, it never could come better.

LIVIA.   You missed your fortunes when you met with her, sir. Young gentlemen that only love for beauty, they love not wisely; such a marriage rather proves the destruction of affection. It brings on want, and want's the key of whoredom. I think you had small means with her?

LEANTIO.   Oh, not any, lady.

LIVIA.   Alas, poor gentleman! What mean'st thou, sir, quite to undo thyself with thine own kind heart? Thou art too good and pitiful to woman. Thank thy lucky stars for this blest fortune that rids the summer of thy youth so well from many beggars that had lain a-sunning in thy beams only else till thou hadst wasted the whole days of thy life in heat and labour. What would you say now to a creature found as pitiful to you as it were even sent on purpose from the whole sex general to requite all that kindness you have shown to it?

LEANTIO.   What's that, madam?

LIVIA.   Could'st thou love such a one that, blow all fortunes, would never see thee want? Nay, more, maintain thee to thine enemy's envy? And shalt not spend a care for it, stir a thought, nor break a sleep — unless love's music waked thee, no storm of fortune should. Look upon me, and know that woman.

LEANTIO.   Oh, my life's wealth, Bianca!

LIVIA.   He's vexed in mind. I came too soon to him. Where's my discretion now, my skill, my judgement? I'm cunning in all arts but my own love. [She goes out]

LEANTIO.   Is she my wife till death, yet no more mine? Methinks by right I should not now be living, and then 'twere all well! She's gone forever — utterly! There is as much redemption as a soul from hell as a fair woman's body from his palace! Why should my love last longer than her truth? What is there good in woman to be loved when only that which makes her so has left her? My safest course, for health of mind and body is to turn my heart and hate her, most extremely hate!

LIVIA [returning].   I have tried all ways I can, and have not power to keep from sight of him. How are you now, sir?

LEANTIO.   I feel a better ease, madam....

LIVIA.   You never saw the beauty of my house yet, nor how abundantly fortune has blessed me. I have enough, sir, to make my friend a rich man in my life, a great man at my death. If you want anything and spare to speak, troth, I'll condemn you for a wilful man, sir.

LEANTIO.   Why sure, this can be but the flattery of some dream....

LIVIA.   Now, by this kiss, my love, my soul, my riches, 'tis all true substance. Take what you list, the gallanter you go, the more you please me, but to me only sir, wear your heart of constant stuff. Do but you love enough, I'll give enough.

Scene Eight

The Palace. CARDINAL and DUKE and BIANCA.

CARDINAL. You vowed never to keep a strumpet more, and are you now so swift in your desires to knit your honours and your life fast to her? Must marriage, that immaculate robe of honour, be now made the garment of leprosy and foulness? Is this penitence, to sanctify hot lust?

DUKE. The path now I tread, is honest. I vowed no more to keep a sensual woman — 'tis done. I mean to make a lawful wife of her.

CARDINAL. Do not grow too cunning for your soul, good brother! Is it enough to use adulterous thefts, and then take sanctuary in marriage?

BIANCA. Sir, I have read you over all this while in silence, and I find great knowledge in you, and severe learning; yet 'mongst all your virtues I see not charity written, which some call the first born of religion, and I wonder I cannot see it....

DUKE. I kiss thee for that spirit! Thou hast praised thy wit a modest way! [He turns back to CARDINAL] Here y'are bitter without cause, brother. What I vow, I keep safe as you your conscience. All this needs not. I taste more wrath in it than I do religion, and envy more than goodness.... [CARDINAL goes out]

BIANCA. How strangely woman's fortune comes about! This was the farthest way to come to me that knew me born in Venice and there with many jealous eyes brought up. 'Tis not good, in sadness, to keep a maid so strict in her young days. Restraint breeds wandering thoughts. I'll never use any girl of mine so strictly — however they're kept, their fortunes find 'em out.

LEANTIO [entering beneath her window]. I long to see how my despiser looks now she's come here to court; these are her lodgings! I took her out of no such window, I remember, first. That was a great deal lower, and less carved....

BIANCA. How now, what silkworm's this, in the name of pride! What, is it he? Methinks you are wondrous brave, sir!

LEANTIO. A sumptuous lodging!

BIANCA. You have an excellent suit, there.

LEANTIO. A chair of velvet!

BIANCA. Is your coat lined through, sir? Who's your shoemaker? He has made you a neat boot.

LEANTIO. Will you have a pair? The duke will lend you spurs.

BIANCA. Yes, when I ride.

LEANTIO. 'Tis a brave life you lead.

BIANCA. I could never see you in such good clothes in my time.

LEANTIO. In your time?

BIANCA. Sure, I think, sir, we both thrive best asunder.

LEANTIO. Y'are a whore.

BIANCA. Oh, sir, you give me thanks for your captainship. I thought you had forgot all your good manners.

LEANTIO. And to spite thee as much, look there, there read! Vex! Gnaw! Thou shalt find there I am not pitiless but there was ever still more charity found out than at one proud fool's door.

BIANCA. Y'are simply happy, sir, yet I'll not envy you.

LEANTIO. No, court-saint, not thou! You keep some friend of a new fashion. There's no harm in your devil, he's a suckling, but he will breed teeth shortly, will he not?

BIANCA. Take heed you play not then too long with him.

LEANTIO. Why, here's sin made and never a conscience put to it! Why do I talk to thee of sense or virtue that art as dark as death? To an ignorance darker than thy womb I leave thy perjured soul. A plague will come!

PART TWO

Scene One

LEANTIO, undressed.

LEANTIO.   We fuck the day to death. And suffocate the night with tossing.
Time stands still, she says so. Rolls back, even. As for the bed, it's
our whole territory, the footboard and the headboard are the horizons of
our estate, rank with the flood of flesh. Oh, beautiful odour of the
utter fuck! And come? No, never come, for that's to end it. Clerks
come, and butchers prior to a good night's kipping, farmers with their
eight strokes, who's not heard their mechanistic butting? I know, was I
not a clerk myself, and salesman? Oh, the bars and barmaids of the
provinces, dead minds spewing the dead opinion, dead eyes on the dying bra
strap slipping **Fuck all that watery desire** no woman under forty is worth
entering! [LIVIA enters] Did I hurt you? For one moment I thought I
have killed her. We do strive in one another, all bruises and dragged
hair....

LIVIA.   You hurt me, and I welcome the hurt. I thought once, I am dying,
and I did not mind. I have no indignation left, surprise, or petty
reservation. No thing I won't yield up, nor thought ashamed to utter.
May I tell you, I have never wanted to be free of you. All other men I
thought, enough, roll off and leave my premises. The ecstasy of being
left, silence and the reclamation of myself. Not you, though. It's five
days since we stepped outside. Are there still streets, and what colour
are the buses? [She looks out the window] Oh, people look the same! Two
legs and heads down, the shuffle and the stagger, **Repetition of the
mundane life!** [She selects among the crowd] She'll lend a little of her
hip, he'll tamper with a giggle, that one might yield her place to satisfy
persistence, and him mutter as he shudders but **Transformation...!** [She
turns back to LEANTIO] **Yes I am arrogant.** Do you complain about my
arrogance? You made me so, and I might have died unknowing....

LEANTIO [at the window].   There has been change here! Look, they paint
the lamp posts for the royal wedding!

LIVIA.   All this bunting clinging to a dirty world! And look, Bianca is
silver paint staring in our bedroom! I heard no workmen hammering!

LEANTIO.   The bitch reviles me! Close the shutter!

LIVIA.   Even in paint, her ambitious lip....

LEANTIO.   And they applaud her, call her innocence!

LIVIA.   You never touched her womb, Leantio. Had you done so she could not
revile you without wanting you as well. Revile and clamour, clamour and
revile. Tell me you don't feel her still, she could give you nothing but
shallow prodding, you could not thrust against her heart like you do mine,
I promise you.

LEANTIO [going to her].   I am slave and master to you alone. Above you I
struggle with a girl, beneath I submit to the hag who lurks inside your
creases, who has not possessed you! Tell me your fuck history, you used
and used again whore —

LIVIA.   He abuses me....

LEANTIO.   Yes! And by abuse I praise you, lavish bitch, hunted and
devoured female —

LIVIA.   Are we insane? I think it possible we are insane!

LEANTIO.   Yes, and good riddance to their sense, their swop of stale
banalities!

LIVIA.   I would not be a girl again —

LEANTIO.   So every woman of your ripeness should say, who finds her match at last! [He kneels to her] Recite to me, who lay in you before me, scratch your memory! [He kisses her belly] I suffer on you, you are my cross, the pain, you know the pain do you, you are a rack also to stretch me on....

LIVIA.   Yes, all you know, I do too....

LEANTIO [stops].   But I do hate Bianca. I wish I could be happy to despise, but no, I hate....

LIVIA.   Good! Hate!

LEANTIO.   Must I?

LIVIA.   Those whose love runs deep dispense no charity. You are no bridegroom whose handshake is free to all, and I no bride all teeth. Through pain of longing we have trod down sickening conviviality. Shudder, shudder at behaviour I tinkled over once. I tinkled then, I did not laugh, and now I find, laughter! Real laughter! Don't suffer shame for proper hates....

LEANTIO.   Your brother wants me dead.

LIVIA.   My brother! Whose tender honour bruises so! Oh, my honour, my sister is a bint for fucking with the factor! The man's a snob, and coarse for all his culture! Listen — [She draws him to her] The world hates passion. Fornication's all its taste, what's good for telling over dinner, how the empty girl was taken, and she smiles, she smiles in willing collaboration, the used smiling at her usage! [She releases him, turns away] And I tried to tell him! **Absurd undertaking!** [She laughs] Such was his contempt I feared he'd chain me as a lunatic! They think of love as discharge, something in the groin to be delivered, I know them, I do know, did I not giggle over their thin and sour longings? **Hunger!** What do they know of that? Touch me and I know I live! [He caresses her] Beloved man, if you perished tonight in some backstreet stabbing, I would say even this little was enough, this was light and transformation. It made me hate my life. All hate your lives and change the world!

Scene Two

THE DUKE, THE CARDINAL, observing.

DUKE.   She is so old....

CARDINAL.   Gone forty, yes....

DUKE.   I think our officers, however lowly, ought not to scandalize us with weird appetites. Can't he speak to girls?

CARDINAL.   I couldn't say.

DUKE.   Bianca was a torment to him.

CARDINAL.   Really?

DUKE.   She tells me he was done before she started.

CARDINAL.   Is that so....

DUKE.   Mind you, they all say that, I won't tell you the cuckolds I've heard denigrated....

CARDINAL [aside].   Stop your philandering, I said. Stop this endless fingering of flesh. I said the public do not like to see this in their governor, but they do! I was wrong there. Profoundly wrong. Who rips the sheets with him, and who was grappled half way down the stairs is all public speculation, keeps the masses warm with itching. It's the entertainment of the modern state and the proper function of an aristocracy! No, carry on, I was wrong to reprimand him! There, church dignitary bows to insatiable appetite of prince... [He bows] There is another sex, however....

DUKE.   I have never touched a woman over thirty! Not knowingly. Fifteen is best. They gasp in wonder, don't dare speak, eyes all big, half terror and half vanity!

CARDINAL.   I think there is another sex, however....

DUKE.   What? I've done it all. [He turns to THE CARDINAL] Is there some posture I've not tried? Some practise of the Arabs you in your dusty library have uncovered? **Banned books!** [He laughs] I assure you this

is something I also have researched. Look at me, brother, fifty-five, and
no part of a girl's anatomy I'm not versed in.   Can place my finger
blindfold and make them shudder at a licking.
CARDINAL.   Yes, I do not doubt it, though this I think is not to do with
posture or with bringing off, but something else.
DUKE.   What, then?
CARDINAL.   Something which unlocks the discipline of the civil state.
DUKE.   Go on.
CARDINAL.   Let all the population copulate, seduce daughters, bring out the
waywardness of wives, whelps and growls from upper storeys all night long,
good, satisfaction and quiescence everywhere, but this might lever up
whole pavements and turn the fountains red.   [He walks a little, stops]
You see, it does not lead to childbirth, which by responsibility, might
modulate its strength....
DUKE.   Oh, come on, stuff your theological euphemisms, what is it, sodomy?
CARDINAL.   I don't know yet....
DUKE.   Whatever it may be, I've done it.
CARDINAL.   Perhaps, I am celibate, and imagine union more immaculate than
actually it is.   That two might lock, and in locking, undo whole cliffs of
discipline seems to me possible....
DUKE.   The fevered fantasy of the deprived.   Dear brother, you stick to
politics.
CARDINAL.   **But it is, you see. It is politics.**   [The DUKE looks at
him, with contempt. Then returns to his observations]
DUKE.   He dotes upon her, licks the experience out of her wrinkles. And
there are girls tight in their skin on every pavement!

Scene Three

THE WARD 's garden.

WARD.   I do love to be in a garden!   To poke my head among the flowers and
make my hair a roost for doves!   I do!   I do!   Sing me a song, there's a
good bitch.   [He sits]   Am I nice and tame?   I have not been out three
weeks for cricket, hunting or the like, have not tumbled headlong off the
horse and staggered home all shit and brandy, have I?   I am the model
husband.   Sing him a song, he is an idiot.   Do you love your idiot?
ISABELLA.   You are not advised to call yourself an idiot or –
WARD.   I shall be taken for one!   Horror!   Stack me in the summerhouse,
prop me like a deckchair stiff against the wall, or do you have a better
use for it?   The summerhouse?   By the way your breath smells. And only
three weeks on the nuptials!   Don't neglect yourself or I may lose my
fascination with you.
ISABELLA.   What fascination? You mean pinching my arse? Your fascination
consists entirely in pulling up my skirt and whooping.
WARD.   Yes, it does and all!   I am an idiot!   Lock me in the summerhouse!
Or do you have another use for it?   I do miss Sordido! I love the doves,
I love the clematis, but Sordido was good to sit with in a storm and watch
the lightning.   I do think sitting with your legs apart is not the way to
charm me.   I mention it in passing.
ISABELLA.   Oh, he cares for my legs, how they face the world!
WARD.   I'm not the world, beloved....
ISABELLA.   I don't require you stay by me. Please, to your clubs and bars
by all means.
WARD.   No, no!   A man who marries must enjoy the woman not only in the
night but in all the glitter of her personality!   Is it tedious to be
married to an idiot?
ISABELLA [darkly].   I am not married to one.
WARD [dark in turn].   No, indeed, but the wife of...?   [He stares at
her, and suddenly, clowns]   Catstick!   Catstick!   [He stops again]   I
think it is a dirty world, where we are stuck together by some senile whim
which thinks our youth will match their sentiments, and our fucking
lubricate their arid transactions.   [She looks at him, amazed]

Catstick!   Catstick!   [He shudders]   I do not like you, you are full of grimy sweetness, like a toffee left in pockets....
ISABELLA.   You do not need to be the child to me. The fat boy. Do you? You do not....
WARD.   Show us yer bum, do!   [She turns, goes out]   I find my only comfort in the mocking of their shallow ardours. I could no more dance attention on these frills and bustles than shove my hand straight to the wet mouth of their hips, **I do like women with a terrible liking but they are not actual, are they?**   [He pretends to recall]   Went down to the river with Sordido once, out of the city in the summer and saw a woman on the bank who looked — in simple cloth dress —looked at me, and I hung there, hung back until she wound me in with her desire like something on a hook, closer and closer I went, wordless to her lips, by the washing basket and the scrubbing brush, she found me straight and I found her, no diversion, up to her heart I reached while Sordido lit a pipe beneath the tree and at the finish she went shh, finger to the lips as if words or gratitude would spoil it, as if to speak would bring sin to its purity....
[Pause]   True story....   [Pause]   **True like fuck it is.**   [He roars with contemptuous laughter. SORDIDO bounds in]
SORDIDO.   She hurries to her uncle, why?
WARD.   Her uncle, why?
SORDIDO.   I can't think why!
WARD/SORDIDO.   **Oh, why, oh, why!**   [They jerk their pelvises in a ritual]
WARD [embracing him].   I have missed you! I can say in utter honesty, in perfect truth, in sworn and honourable veracity so help me God I longed for your foul observations, did I not!
SORDIDO.   Truth? Truth? A perfect truth, what's that?
WARD [pointing to the floor].   **Saw one!**
SORDIDO.   Truth, oi!
WARD [diving].   Caught it! Down you bugger!
SORDIDO.   Net! Net!
WARD.   Slippery...slippery....
SORDIDO [pretending to grapple with invisibility].   Says — says —
WARD [cupping his ear].   What?
SORDIDO.   Squeaks.... **Nice — place — you — got.**   [He releases it]
WARD.   She brought money. She brought flesh. With one tit in my paw I glance across the garden which is designed according to my whim, shape of the dollar enclosing female lip, the box tree is the dollar and the geraniums the lip, and I think where is my mate, his squalid den? And lo, he bounds into my presence. I hate all, and the more I have, the more I hate, especially old men, them I would kill. Women less, they are farcical merely. The duke prods bossy virgins and they think, bliss, oh, bliss, **What is bliss exactly?** I thought of hanging myself with a tennis net, to carry my act to the end, my funeral would be the gladdest event in the social calendar... [SORDIDO puts his arm around him] Shall we do a murder? Shall we strangle Isabella, or the uncle, in some shuddering copulation up against the summerhouse? That appeals to me, but no, it would be taken as a vengeance, as if I cared who shagged her place! I have not entered her, but laid beside her, irritatingly. Have you yet?
SORDIDO.   What?
WARD.   Been with a woman?
SORDIDO.   Never, as you know.
WARD.   Explains their hunger of you, as if by restraint some unknown power's gathered in your parts. It's cruelty! You being rather dirty and rather handsome, two things they stir for in collaboration, they almost whimper as you pass **What is bliss** it's murder, surely?
SORDIDO.   Here comes all we loathe, and all we loathe in its company....
FABRITIO.   Good news! Good news!
WARD.   **'O says yer can waddle in my garden!**   [GUARDIANO and FABRITIO enter] THE WARD bows a mocking greeting]   Hatred of age... Hatred of age....
FABRITIO.   Good news!
WARD.   You don't have a key, do you? Walking in on us, I might be in your

daughter's frills and then what? Tact! Tact! Under the meandering bees, sticky fingered and arse-rampant! Tact! Tact!

FABRITIO [wounded].   You were less coarse-spoken prior to the matrimonial....

WARD.   I was less used. I find stacks of vocabulary in my humiliation. Well, humiliation they call it who know me not, among them I count you, beloved guardian, who spent my loot and in cruel boarding houses got me off your back, and you believed my school report I was the dunce!

GUARDIANO.   You were! It said so! And you behaved it well enough!

WARD.   A proper love would see through a malicious schoolboy's pain.

GUARDIANO.   I had such business to attend to I —

WARD.   **Catstick!**

GUARDIANO.   The responsibilities of the estate —

WARD.   **Cat — stick!** [Pause. GUARDIANO concedes] My dead parent who enabled me this prettiness the Turks strung across a rigging, tongue out, guts out, genitalia ripped up by the roots, most appropriate, Christian trader, Christian money-hunter, would have swopped his bowel for a dollar, but must admire them, the spirit of adventure, **Spirit of adventure it was avarice,** for coming home and buying cunt in furs, this man knows adventure — [He indicates SORDIDO] this is the great adventurer, who never strays from Florence and her gutters, this is the great explorer, the immaculate cartographer of human vice, stuff your funny tribes and exotic animals, your zoos and exhibitions, **All beasts live in Florence, I know, they clamber on my back.** [He nudges SORDIDO] Describe our fauna, you know them best.

SORDIDO [examining FABRITIO and GUARDIANO].   Here, for your inspection, two common specimens, adult and mature, in plumage of the mating season—

GUARDIANO.   I do not see why we —

WARD.   **Respect his genius.**

GUARDIANO.   Should be subjected to —

WARD.   **His genius. His wit.** [Pause. GUARDIANO acts patience]

SORDIDO.   The mating season which is not a season but is permanent, stamping their webbed feet on the ground as signal of peculiar distress make calls thus, 'My dignity! My dignity!', a somewhat ugly cry and beaks a-quiver with olfactory obsession with tail feathers of the female. Relation to the European magpie, pica pica, has huge appetite for silver, with which it lines its rather squalid nest, and flocks about midday to the exchange, making the repeated call of 'profit, profit, profit!' until with onset of the feeding hour, which occupies all afternoon, it makes its graceless flight to overstocked barns leaking dung —

GUARDIANO.   All right, all right —

SORDIDO.   Most unedifying spectacle, the life cycle of this parasitic bird —

GUARDIANO.   Childish —

FABRITIO.   Infantile —

GUARDIANO.   Repetition of stale ideology.... [He walks a little way, then pointedly] What a beautiful garden....

WARD [embracing SORDIDO].   He knows everything, and has not strolled beyond the river...what brings you here? And what's bliss, I long to know....

FABRITIO.   You have bliss in your bedroom if I know it.

WARD.   What, my wife? He calls bliss a body! They know nothing, this ornithology!

FABRITIO.   I'll rescue her, she'll not stay with a fiend like you who tricked us playing idiot — [THE WARD feints to butt him] Hit me! Dare you? Hit me!

WARD.   No, I shan't crack your eggshell, vain old sparrow, shan't give you the satisfaction, though to strike old men is not offensive to my values....

GUARDIANO.   We'll end our visit here, and tell you plain and dry what should have been cause for celebration. The Duchess of Florence, soon to be, has chosen your abused young wife as maid at her wedding. Now, you see, a great honour we thought to bring with love you've wrecked with spite and barracking.

FABRITIO [in angry tears].   Yes, knife-mouth!   And she'll not lie with
you if I'm her father!
SORDIDO.   He don't in any case, except to pinch her bum when she is
sleeping.   Now, buzz!

He swings a kick at FABRITIO, and follows them off menacingly.   ISABELLA
appears from cover, staring after them.

ISABELLA.   Peculiar parenthood, that gladly sells me to an idiot, but
finding he has mind, is all a-scuttle to rescue me....   [She turns to THE
WARD]   Talk to me....
WARD.   Never.
ISABELLA.   Lie with me, then.   Now, in the sunshine, throw the window open
and turn back the sheet.   Tell.   Do tell.

Scene Four

The Palace.   THE MOTHER and BIANCA.

MOTHER.   I was a widow, having been the good wife to a man not very
passionate.   Loyal, though not without temptation.   For forty years bred
children and clean shirts.   Pride in polish.   Honour in starch.   And now,
on the rim of the grave I see — **The riot of lost possibilities!**   [She
weeps] Oh, roll back the hours, toss off the years!   Give me my luscious
breasts back, I was robbed....
BIANCA.   You have your compensations, surely?   Though I can't lay words to
them.
MOTHER.   Oh shut up, you well-fucked thing.   All I can draw to me are
scabby, legless soldiers and they would dare to call me hag....
BIANCA.   Tell you what!   On your grave I'll have inscribed the one word
Honesty.   How's that?
MOTHER.   Arrogant bitch.
BIANCA.   No!   I'll have the mason chip **She cooked for five.**   How's that?
MOTHER.   Mock on, juvenile, your eyes won't pull forever...
BIANCA.   Or better still, **Here lay the cleanest carpet in all Florence.**
MOTHER.   Piss.
BIANCA.   I wound you only to endorse myself.   The little conscience
lurked, did most certainly, until your son abused me.   Then I saw, under
his little charm lay hatred.   Undo the rope of love just once and like a
sack of dead and rancid cats all stench pours over your knees and feet.   I
think men do not like us, though they sweat with wanting, or if they like
us, can't fuck except with jogging fondness.   No love without hate.
That's my discovery to date.   Correct me if I'm wrong.   Does that accord
with your experience?
MOTHER.   How would I know....   Rather a punch in a sodden bedroom than what
I got.
DUKE [entering].   Oh, your best friend weeping!
BIANCA.   Yes, for all the phantoms she would not embrace.
DUKE.   I'm not a phantom, embrace me!
MOTHER.   I dare not, for some smothered feeling might uncoil....
DUKE.   God forbid!
MOTHER [to BIANCA].   Kiss him, do, I bow down to your ambition....my
idiot boy would have worked all hours to get you half a knicker you now
toss to the servants from a single wearing...fondle her, she is perfect,
she is ruthless, more so than you....
DUKE.   And she cannot get enough of me!
MOTHER.   Today....
BIANCA.   Yes, I am mad for him, and it's not to do with dresses, nor with
dinners neither —
MOTHER.   No, no...!
BIANCA.   It's not!   He draws me, look at him.   He is a manly man, who makes
a woman proud, and after, weak.   Strong to be loved by him, and a puddle
for his desires....

MOTHER.   Excellent. And yet he's ugly. Begging your indulgence. By all
we thought in my day. But so what? He's ugly.
DUKE.   I am not ugly. I am the Duke.
MOTHER.   He is the Duke.
DUKE.   No duke is ugly. I could go like the lice-infested tramp, all
fingers in the arm pits, and assure you, all the blades would call it
fashion and go scratching likewise, and all women would say, how well he
scratches, he is the essence of manhood!
BIANCA [crossly].   It is not so!
DUKE [placatory].   No, no, indeed....
BIANCA.   You humble your fineness, you — [HIPPOLITO enters. She turns
to him, bewildered] It is not so, surely, that he is — worth five
mundane husbands, surely?
HIPPOLITO.   Ten, if yours is fit to go by.
MOTHER.   How does he go, my old discarded boy? Often at his castle? He
don't invite me ever.
HIPPOLITO.   My sister is a fool for him. They carry their joint lechery
into the street when they snatch time from the bedroom.
DUKE [mocking].   In the street! That you would never do! No, sir,
discretion is your prime quality.
HIPPOLITO.   I do my best.
DUKE.   Who would know, to look at him, his neck had travelled through his
niece's skirts? Not me, sir!
HIPPOLITO.   I'm sorry you find something comical in caution. I shall enjoy
my treasure without taking her against the alley wall.
DUKE.   Wall-fucking! And the woman is forty!
HIPPOLITO.   I think we understand, notionally at least, the power of the
oligarchy rests on respect —
DUKE.   Respect, is it?
HIPPOLITO.   Respect, yes, which is not wall-fucking, is it?
BIANCA.   They are in love....
HIPPOLITO.   Me, too. But if all love to be believed must entail straddling
in public —
DUKE.   **Respect? Respect?** Nay, stuff respect. It's violence. Pageantry
and violence.
HIPPOLITO.   You phrase it nakedly.
DUKE.   Why not? I tell you how we govern. Tinsel to the nostrils and a
spike at the arse.   [HIPPOLITO bows]   He looks affronted!   Oh, the
tasteful man, and he reads books! Hippolito is chock with wisdom, and
when he dies, will do it quietly, as he fucks, secure in the knowledge all
he did was done with taste and judgement, never coarse and never loud....
[He entertains] It is not fair! Is it? Not fair! Some men succeed at
everything! I have a mind to glance at Isabella. Where does he keep his
clandestine wife?
BIANCA.   You dare go sniffing at her skirt —
DUKE.   A mind, I said, I have a mind —
BIANCA.   Great bastard, I would hack thy organ — [She advances on him]
MOTHER.   I think, seeing the way they go on here, it was a simple crew
down at the tavern, and I thought them gross when they swore fuck...no,
they had no evil such as yours.
DUKE.   Drivel, they merely lacked the leisure to refine their lust.
Hippolito, you be best man at my marriage.
HIPPOLITO.   I thank you, that great honour.
DUKE.   And help pay for it!
HIPPOLITO.   I thank you for that honour also.
DUKE.   He thanks me all the time. All this gratitude, first sign of
treason.
HIPPOLITO.   Never. I'm of your party.
DUKE.   Of it? Squire, you made it! We were shit but one decade ago,
forever in the courts of bankruptcy! Now kiss me, and don't get murdered
by the opposition. [HIPPOLITO kisses his cheek] My popularity was never
higher, and she dangles from me, flashing like some encrusted gem,
blinding discontent and dazzling the cynic. Duchess of Florence! How
does the title please you?

BIANCA.   It enhances my beauty.

DUKE.   It does so, and your enhanced beauty in turn enhances me. It would not have troubled me were you a laundress with eight bastards, I would have carried you here. I must have beauty.

MOTHER.   Yes, but what is it, this thing beauty?

DUKE.   What it is I couldn't tell you. What it is not I know when I look at you.

MOTHER.   She has a straight nose, and last year curved noses were in....

DUKE [stung].   Stuff your wisdom.   I'll tell you what beauty is, it is what all men collude in desiring, and what all men desire I must have, and fuck it, so there, silence your curiosity with that. [BIANCA looks at him reproachfully]   She forces crudity out of me, and now I am embarrassed, why do you keep her here? [He turns to MOTHER]   You will see, old mother, that the dossers will applaud my wedding and go home warmer than they would be from a meal, there is great nourishment in pageantry. Later, the royal birth will have them gasping who cannot conceive themselves, and those that can will name their stinking brats after ours immaculate.... [He goes to BIANCA]   Why has she not conceived already, she might grow a belly from a kiss so sweet is her saliva and so fecund her red mouth.... [They gaze at one another]

HIPPOLITO.   I'll come back later for the details of the wedding....

MOTHER.   Be off and leave us.... I could watch for hours, like staring at a living picture book.... [THE CARDINAL enters, and watches]

CARDINAL.   The service says, which I have recited over the bowed heads of the betrothed a thousand times and always wondered at it, 'with my body I thee worship'.   What says the Almighty to this other faith?   Is he not a jealous god?   What worship is it?   Can you tell?

MOTHER.   Shh!

CARDINAL.   It is comprehensible, I do insist!

BIANCA [detaching herself].   You would have scientists put microscopes to women's breasts and weigh them in the scales, and come out only with the circumference or gravity, not one smatter wiser why it drives a prince to melancholic death he cannot touch them.   Mystery!   Adore it!   There is little enough and it eases my journey through this puddle of dead dreams to know a man might murder for me, just as when I grow loose on my skeleton like her, to know no man will spare me half a glance will help me say, so, time I quit, and make death easy.

DUKE.   Hooray!   She owns all the words, and all the juices, marvel at her, moist and brilliant bitch, she cuts the air with phrases, then seduces it!

CARDINAL.   She is most philosophical for seventeen....

BIANCA.   No, I only repeat what clergy tell me, that we all swill in sin. I have trod by beggars and thought, not, oh, charity, oh, alms, but oh, fragility of consciousness, give me a man who finds me in all this horror — divine!

Scene Five

The street. LIVIA.

LIVIA [gazing about her].   This hogheap.   The ratpile.   This dosserdom. The hand goes from mouth, to genital, to arse. Fill, rub, and wipe. The geometry of servile continuation.   And yet — in all of them I think the possibility of ridiculing the meanness of God's gift, of yelling to his paucity, I chuck off the three points of my loneliness, I will not be animal but ecstasy!

HIPPOLITO [entering, taking her roughly by the arm].   There you are, come off the alley —

LIVIA.   Don't handle me, I am lecturing the universe —

HIPPOLITO.   You expose the madness in yourself, you were better plotting liaisons in the parlour.

LIVIA.   Well, I fixed you up, how is your fingering?   I will not flatter it by a better title — **You hurt.**

HIPPOLITO.   What are you to criticize?   You know nothing of our passage.

LIVIA.   I do.   I see you are the man you were.   Therefore your love is drivel.

HIPPOLITO.   I loathe your arrogance — your breast is out!

LIVIA.   It is...!   Don't dare replace it, or cover the adored and worshipped thing.   It fills him with wonder, for all its papery and worn contour, see, it reads you its history, it is no girl's balloon.

HIPPOLITO.   Madness!   You have come apart somewhere —

LIVIA.   Well, yes, all over!

HIPPOLITO.   I need but a pair of signatures and you can be transported to a high and ventilated room where nuns will rope you to a bed.   I need but two doctor's signatures.

LIVIA.   A doctor's signature!   I think there is nothing cheaper, or more willingly lent to the state.   Look, there goes a doctor, hey!   This woman has found a proper use for her — down here, sir — write on a paper she has caught some terrible employment for her — down here, sir — **Don't say the word** — it's a thing for making soldiers for the state — [to HIPPOLITO] **If you had known desire you would not look at me like that.**   [Pause] Dear brother, I think you are utterly corrupt, as I was once, and if I'm mad, it's only health to be so.   I fling off all the junk of sitting rooms that eased me slowly to a sickening retirement.   I am utterly alive, and flow where once I rattled dry as straw on saltmarsh, truly....

HIPPOLITO.   I do not know you, sister, and wish I did.   Those afternoons bathed in the fountain of your wit, you teased all of society, and every hit was centre....

LIVIA.   Teased it, yes, but altered it?   I would not go to my grave with such an epitaph as this — she had her salon, she had her wit, she had her teacups and her gin.   No, I loathe wit, the rattle of dry words and poets licking one another's sisters.   I think we lived an elegant and disgusting life.

HIPPOLITO.   We?   We?   I smell him on your clothes!

LIVIA.   Yes!

HIPPOLITO [seizing her again].   I cannot witness this!   This rotting of a woman!   [They struggle.   SORDIDO appears]

SORDIDO.   Oi!   You gents make too much noise.   Get gone.   [HIPPOLITO looks at SORDIDO, hesitates, goes]   Mrs, you are well-loved, I can see it....

LIVIA.   Yes, but for most of mankind it renders me comprehensible as a dumb Arab....

SORDIDO.   A stranger even, catches it, some signal like the sailors' flags which read 'I come well satisfied....'

LIVIA.   It's true, and who are you, unnecessarily ragged, feigning the artisan?   What are you, a graduate in some obscure science?   It won't do in this state to parade your education.   Learning, like love, is for the sewers.

SORDIDO.   It's the sewers that I live in.

LIVIA.   When all above is poison, the sweetest things must flourish in old cracks....

SORDIDO [looking around].   Please, this is the gutter we are standing in, and cops all around us dressed as men — [He performs spontaneously] **Long live the Duke!   The Duke a wondrous man, adore the duke there!   Adore him you bastard!   Roll on his nuptials, etcetera!**   He has a big cock, did you know it?   Shh!   I also pretend to be mad.

LIVIA.   I like you.   You are not innocent.

SORDIDO.   I am made for the age.   I carry my brains in my fingers and write nothing.   All knowledge lies in instinct, the fugitive carries the truth behind his teeth, don't lend me a book I will be spotted, **Man with a book there!**   [He smiles]   Now sleep with me, if I have entertained you.   This offer comes exclusive, since I was a man I've done no more than kiss, and that but faintly....

LIVIA.   Entertained me, yes you have, but the other, thanks I will not.

SORDIDO.   Oh, mingey loyalty to some idle cove, I hate that.

LIVIA.   Not loyalty, but hunger for one only, that's proper chastity.   I swear nothing to priests or civil servants.

SORDIDO.   He has worked wonders on you....

LIVIA.   And me on him. I'm not his instrument. And yet I am.
SORDIDO.   Unfair world, he muttered ritually....
LIVIA.   No democracy in love.
SORDIDO.   None, and I'm no democrat. The word stinks like fish forgotten
on the slab.   This wedding will drive me to a murder — [He performs
again] **Long live the duke! His charm, his love of fun! Adore him you
mean-minded bastard!** The more democracy is clapping the more I feel some
growl start here — [He indicates his stomach] and all my cheeks aswamp
with bilious acid, swallow, swallow, choke!
LIVIA.   It was not arbitrary, your coming across.
SORDIDO.   How could it be? In this state we are all linked who hate, by
little quirks and signs, and eyes to eyes direct when looking down would
be collusion with the great unanimous approval. The word which charac-
terizes everything is **Yes** and no is only fit for whispering — [He
grabs a passer-by by his lapels] Say yes!
MAN.   Yes....
SORDIDO.   He says it! See! [He turns back to LIVIA] You are a no, or
you could not fuck like that... good day....

He bows. LIVIA goes off. BIANCA and THE MOTHER appear, indulging a crowd.
LEANTIO also, suddenly from a new direction.

LEANTIO.   Hide me, sir!
SORDIDO.   Turn edgeways then, I'm not broad.
LEANTIO.   Hide me and later I'll explain it.
SORDIDO.   No, use me do and fuck explanation.
LEANTIO.   Is that the duchess of the state?
SORDIDO.   In everything but title....
LEANTIO.   Hide me!
SORDIDO.   I do, I do, but I must breathe out and naturally I shrink a
little...there, I puff up... [They stare at BIANCA]
LEANTIO.   She goes — what does she do — tell me —
SORDIDO.   Shopping.
LEANTIO.   Shopping, why? She needs nothing.
SORDIDO.   What's need to do with shopping?
LEANTIO.   She forever decks herself out....
SORDIDO.   I hear beneath it all she has a body but none's seen it....
LEANTIO.   Who says?
SORDIDO.   She is a virgin, sir. The paper says so.
LEANTIO.   Look! The poor go ahh, go ahh, go ahh...she is pretty, they are
poor, she grins and they go ahh....
SORDIDO.   The acme of artificiality.
LEANTIO.   No, she means it, which is worse.... Turn! She comes by here!
SORDIDO.   I charge for this, most mobile tree trunk. Forgive me, I must
clap, I have my act to think of.... [He applauds BIANCA, who smiles,
passes]
LEANTIO.   They simper at her beauty, but what do they think?
SORDIDO [darkly].   They see her naked in their mind's eye....
LEANTIO.   No, they think her pure, they cannot envisage such whiteness on
its back and yelping.
SORDIDO [staring after BIANCA].   You imagine with authority.
LEANTIO.   Her love is crude. Is crude, I tell you. [They watch her
depart] There, she clears off leaving the rabble disputing in their rags
which bonnet suits her best, like fifty popes had sprayed their misery
with water.... [He turns to SORDIDO] I thank you. I was seeking my
mistress who went out only for some oranges....
SORDIDO.   I understand your impatience. Was she smooth and clear-eyed,
full of pride in body? It stands out miles, this quality....
LEANTIO.   Yes. Are you much experienced with women?
SORDIDO.   I've slept with none, but I imagine. [He goes to leave]
LEANTIO.   Wait, you prince of scrim and flannel.... [SORDIDO turns] The
hag was my mother, and the duchess was my wife....
SORDIDO.   It's an offence to say so. None have had relations with her but
the Duke.

LEANTIO.   Well, I tease.... [Pause. Their eyes are locked]
SORDIDO [smiling].   I know it. So much loathing could only come from
ripped-up love. They say a fool brought her from Venice and lost her in a
week. You are the fool.
LEANTIO.   I struggled miserably with the misapprehension she desired me.
Desire she did not.
SORDIDO.   Desire?   Now that I cannot understand.   You mean she — no
what is it, this desire?   Old men will dribble at her wedding, is that
it? And bollocky youths make crude eyes, ramming out their arses, is that
it?   **And Dukes go thump, thump, thump into her belly, is that it!**
[LEANTIO clasps him round the shoulders, laughing]
LEANTIO.   I think I love you! You hate all, and who else can be trusted
but him who hates with such discrimination?
SORDIDO.   I am Sordido, and you may find me in odd attics scratching with
the dead men, or swallowing fine wines in the horticultural extravaganza
known as Isabella's house.... [LEANTIO starts to go] Plot with me. [He
stops]   I shall burst into the wedding and take the impeccable by force.
My first and only entrance to the gateway of all life and death.   In her
washed matrimonial skin, all scented for the state and bishops'
twittering, I'll force her. Down on some polished marbles in foams of
lace and splitting fabrics I'll fuck her place! [Pause]   There, forget I
spoke.   Only a vision.   I am liable to visions.   Comes of poverty and
weird alcohols.... [LEANTIO is deeply stirred.   He looks long into
SORDIDO, and SORDIDO into him] Sometime your life comes to you in the
street, drops at your feet like birds dead in the frozen winter.   Plop!
The crux of your life. And you were only out for oranges.... [He lingers,
leaves. LIVIA hurries in, eating an orange and carrying a bagful]
LIVIA.   This crowd of gaping gobs has separated us! [She kisses him]
The genuflecting poor! And filthy hands applauding riches!   Was there
ever a spectacle more likely to make lovers ashamed of love?   I felt like
smacking them out of their servility. [She holds out the bag]   Oranges.
[He does not take one]
LEANTIO.   I met a man...
LIVIA.   I also! Do take one, they are so sweet!
LEANTIO.   And the man chilled me with a dream.
LIVIA.   Look, how huge they are!
LEANTIO [sending the bag flying].   Piss your oranges!   [They roll across
the street. Pause]
LIVIA.   What dream, Leantio? [He stares]
LEANTIO.   A dream not fit for telling.   [He takes her arm]   Let's get to
bed and drown evil in perspiration —
LIVIA.   Wait —
LEANTIO.   Smother me in your hollows —
LIVIA.   Wait, I said —
LEANTIO [turning angrily on her].   Wait, what for! Wait, you, who never
waits?   What is this hanging back, you with your barmy appetite for love,
legs ever open for my fist and now won't shift, why! [Pause]
LIVIA.   My flesh is not a pond to drown your fears in.   [Pause]
Desire's truth, Leantio, and compels it speak.   All the rest is fucking.
Our union is not a place for hiding in, or a sink to vomit temper.
[Pause]   What dream, and who was he?
LEANTIO.   A dream of Bianca raped.   On her wedding morning. [She goes to
him, takes his arm]   I dare not see more of him!   He visits Isabella's
house, or you discover him in cellars, so he says, which cellars do you
think?   A man in black and alive with hate.   **He made me long for
vengeance on the doll who was my wife.** The dying embers of that instinct
he fanned with his imagination, let's go...!
LIVIA.   Find him.
LEANTIO.   Find him?
LIVIA.   The man who shakes you so.   And drag his dream into the
daylight....
LEANTIO [staring at her].   What are you? Livia? [She extends a hand to
him. He does not take it]   Can't...walk beside you but...can't touch....
[She leads off. He follows. As they leave, THE CARDINAL appears,

watching]

CARDINAL.   They walk with space between them. The flesh cool and the veins not hammering...what's done that? [He picks up an orange, contemplatively] An idea...! Oh, God, an idea has come between them! Oh, easy lust or nagging marriage, this we know and manage, but imagination...! **Birth of an idea there!**

Scene Six

The fort at Rouens. A party enters.

LIVIA [mocking].   Here's a fort to terrify an enemy! The walls are thick with ivy and the cannon in the ditch. As for the garrison, it's nettles!

SORDIDO.   Attention, nettles!

LIVIA [to LEANTIO].   I did not know the reach of the Duke's contempt for you until this minute...he might have smacked you for a cuckold, public in the gob, as give you this derogatory honour. Loose stair there!

WARD [gazing around].   Leantio, exquisite appointment! Where will you pitch your pennant? A peasant has the flagpole for fencing cattle in! [Laughter]

LIVIA.   My skirt's his flag, flapping in the foul wind which blows off Florence.   Smell, smell that!   [She breathes in, leaning over the parapet] Stink of the nightclub and brassy odour of the stock exchange!

WARD [breathing deeply].   Duke's crevices.

SORDIDO.   Officers' fart and dying breath of doormen.

LIVIA.   Vomit of the debutante.

SORDIDO.   Great stench of black-gummed deference.

LEANTIO.   Why gather here? Where is the virtue in it? [He turns away]

LIVIA [staring at the distant city].   Look, the city glows in dusk... throbs with the pulse of money...we stand outside it and with one finger eliminate corruption... [She holds up a finger before her eyes]

LEANTIO.   This is a futile picnic, dancing defiance from a distance...

LIVIA [turning away].   But laugh we must! Must laugh at wit of dukes, who give decrepit forts to men with decent grudges!

SORDIDO.   Laugh, yes, because our joke is better.

LEANTIO.   What joke? The ruination of Bianca?

LIVIA.   Ruination, why? We save her.

LEANTIO.   Save her! By rape! Since when was rape salvation?

LIVIA.   Leantio, whole cliffs of lies fall down in storms. By this catastrophe she'll grope for knowledge her ambition hides from her. And simultaneously, Sordido's crime will rock the state off its foundations, which is erected on such lies as ducal marriages.

LEANTIO.   I've hated her, God knows the length of my loathing, yet I would not have my basest urgings played to —

LIVIA.   Oh, he is so decent, forcing down his feelings!

LEANTIO.   What did you love me for?

LIVIA.   **Your hunger. Not your decency.** [She holds him passionately] What we have found in love doesn't come to clerks with consciences, all 'does this please you' and 'forgive me, does that hurt?' No, but taking, from the depths of unkind longing! We liberate her from herself, and at the same stroke, unleash contempt on all we've come to hate.

LEANTIO.   Where is the realism in all this?

LIVIA.   **Realism I hate the word.** [She contains her fury] Shall we, who have come to knowledge and own truth, not act on it? Shall we shrivel up in sarcasms, giggling at the satires of the radicals and make content with sympathizing, doling cash to rebels we're too posh to meet? I have thrown my money to the poor while hating charity, and laughed at criminals while hating crime, and now I act! It kills the soul not to exploit an inspiration! [Pause] Oh, I irritate him with my earnestness! Forgive me, I see enthusiasm welcomed only in bed....

LEANTIO.   Enthusiasm?   Enthusiasm's madness, or its sister, what's enthusiasm doing here?

LIVIA [contemptuously].   Leantio, the clerk...!   The clerk is showing

through the skin....
LEANTIO [stung].   You hate Bianca and dress up revenge as politics!
LIVIA.   Hate her?   No, I pity her.   It's you who hates.
LEANTIO.   Pity?   You?   Pity's not a quality I'd pin to you.
LIVIA.   Pity, yes.   Pity her who uses cunt as property, to buy her way up
floors of privilege.   When Sordido's forced his pain on her she'll learn
the thing she sells can just as well be stolen.... [Pause.   He paces]
LEANTIO.   We rob her of her rights...
SORDIDO.   Her right to nay.   Her right to yea, she can keep that.   [He
paces, turns]
LEANTIO.   This rape — this rape you call deliverance —
SORDIDO.   Rape, indeed, and not the first time....
LEANTIO [turning on SORDIDO].   Who raped her previously, me?
LIVIA.   You?   Never you.   The Duke.   With my connivance.   I wrapped her for
his lust and tied the ribbon, while you sweated in a foreign port.
LEANTIO.   It was seduction, though I shudder to imagine, seduction it was,
surely —
SORDIDO.   **Violation.**   [Pause]   Violation, yes, which came by wealth and
power.   And her protesting mouth was stopped, not by a fist, but greed and
glamour suffocated it.   By her squalid ambition was repulsion choked.   And
now, against the Duke's degraded appetite, my purity claims access to her
ravaged territory.   [Pause.   LEANTIO stares at him]
LEANTIO.   It's death.
SORDIDO.   I risk death for her privacy.   And stealing her toy virginity,
all the poor of Florence grab their rights, who had been meant only to
swoon with insatiable envy....
WARD.   While he, immaculate rebel, among her moist wound intrudes, I'll
shout out **Oh, exquisite robbery!**
LIVIA [laughing, embracing THE WARD].   Here comes your wife, delighted
with this mossy tower and thinking it a perfect place to picnic!
WARD [going to intercept her at the top of the steps].   Beloved!   The
steps are shattered, mind your ankle!
LIVIA.   Through her I will arrange Sordido's entry to the palace.   Hurry,
leave us...!   [SORDIDO and THE WARD hasten down.   LIVIA turns to LEANTIO]
Who would have thought I might descend to trickery again?   Old skills
don't die.   Sad truth.   [She caresses him]   And yet, a thing is vile, not
in itself, but only in relation to its usage —
LEANTIO.   Not so, that's cruel misuse of reason —
LIVIA.   **Of course it's so.**   [He turns from her.   Pause]
LEANTIO.   So, this is the infant of our exceptional love.... You labour
for a child as hideous as this....
LIVIA.   You are so precious, who half-killed me with his passion once....
[Pause.   She takes his head in her hands]   Oh, listen, our love plunged
through all layers of affection, burst longing, split open desire, struck
seams not of comfort but of truth!   We humiliate our long adventure if we
draw back from its message!
ISABELLA [entering].   Oh, pretty place!
LIVIA [disengaging from LEANTIO].   I knew you'd love it!   [She goes to
her side]   Niece, all's well with you if you adore your husband — [She
turns back to LEANTIO]   Do leave us to speak a little, private thing...!
[LEANTIO goes out]   He wants to love you, chaste and passionate, it's
true!   Is he not kind to you, in preparation?   Confirm it, he has not for
whole weeks teased you.
ISABELLA.   No, he has been weird and considerate....
LIVIA.   Exactly!   His scheme — of such excessive romance I could blush
for him — is to marry you at Bianca's wedding!
ISABELLA.   Marry me?   We are already married!
LIVIA.   Oh, that, no, this one he calls proper.   It's the way with these
leathery cynics to want white weddings and lace underthings who bawl the
dirtiest.   [Pause]
ISABELLA.   Two weddings?   One for the mass...one secret....
LIVIA.   Yes!   And this with consummation!   But one thing.   He will have
Sordido there as witness, then to depart, no more the irritation to your
happiness.

ISABELLA.   Sordido....
LIVIA.   Smuggle him in, as Gentlemen to you.   He'll kiss hands and vanish.
You'll hear no more from him.
ISABELLA.   Dear Aunt — [She goes to embrace her. LIVIA recoils]
LIVIA.   No, you only wound me with your gratitude, I merely repeat your
loved one's own suggestions.   Now, downstairs and join them at the
barbecue.... [ISABELLA skips away] Nothing's lost...for all my travelling
in love, through hurricanes of difference...I believe I'm even better at
it....

Scene Seven

The Palace. BIANCA is bridal.

BIANCA [posturing at a mirror].   What do you think?
CARDINAL.   Think....
BIANCA.   To see me thus. Do you think — she is pretty as a doll — she
is so pretty she is — scarcely human — or rather, at some point
she is naked under that? [She walks, turns] Do you think, she is a
confection of femininity, or rather — I would give my life to kiss her
arse? I only ask. I have never been a duchess before.
CARDINAL.   I think — you are not a woman at all — but a symbol of the
state.
BIANCA.   You have a wonderful intellect.
CARDINAL.   I have lived my life with symbols. I am wearing symbols. I
worship them. I finger them before I sleep.
BIANCA.   It is a strange way to spend a life, always the thing that isn't,
and never the thing that is. I think your head must ache. And not just
your head. Ache...ache... [She hurries to him, anxious, proud] Look what
I've done! Look at me! Am I not perfect? Say I'm perfect, you who has
been since his cradle, celibate, tell me I am perfect!
CARDINAL.   In all ways.
BIANCA.   I think this is the absolute of joy! And everything hereafter,
downhill.   After you have anointed us, and all trumpets and all beggars
and all cavalry have pranced and wept and bellowed and spat spit and
coughed phlegm and shat their dung and splintered glasses and all old
women cried for what they never knew and all the ugly railed at what they
never were, I shall on the eiderdown, among cracking of braid and tearing
taffeta, go down for his lips, and all the power of the state will huddle
at my little, florid entrance....
CARDINAL.   The state made flesh....
BIANCA.   There you go — symbols again! Still, if it keeps you sane...
[He turns to go, bowing] You know, I think there must be poverty, if not
of life, then mind. Or we could not love ourselves so much.... [He goes
out. THE MOTHER enters, adoring]
MOTHER.   You dazzle, darling. Brilliance splashing through my cataracts.
If I were a man, I'd say fuck God, why kneel to him, this is perfection.
And it is.... [She weeps]
BIANCA [holding her].   I am everything, aren't I?   I am everything.
There must be me, mustn't there? There must be me, or they would all —
SORDIDO.   Despair? [She turns]
BIANCA.   You mistook your entrance. Chamberlains and ushers in the hall
ISABELLA [entering, crossly].   You should not be here!
SORDIDO.   No, this is my entrance —
ISABELLA.   No, you go — [She goes to lead him]
SORDIDO.   **This is my entrance.**   [He advances on BIANCA] I am so
immaculate for this. I am not some fetid courtier or mortgagee who labels
himself Duke by virtue of some thousand hired guards, no, were he even
half-legitimate he could not quarrel with my right **I am thirty and
pure.** No dirty walls resounded with my roar as I thumped the belly of
the prostitute, am I not good for this, and fit to be your mate? You are
no virgin, after all, I flatter you with my infatuation....
BIANCA [sensing his intention, to ISABELLA].   Fetch my officer, who

stands outside.

SORDIDO.   Drag him in by all means, he has no throat to cry alarm.

ISABELLA [horrified].   **What is this?**

LIVIA [entering].   I must, who makes dreams come to life, witness the occurrence. Don't call my hypocrite, what I have dealt in I attend right to the finish.

MOTHER [recognizing her].   Oh, lady, I know you! We played chess when I was your neighbour!

LIVIA [her eyes fixed on BIANCA].   Is that so?   The moves I don't recall....

BIANCA.   Why are you here?

LIVIA.   Did I not work your seduction by the governor of this place, and now unwork it....

BIANCA.   You tremble...more than me....

LIVIA.   Yes....

BIANCA.   Is this my murder, then?

SORDIDO.   Shout help and see. As for gasps, I make allowances.... [He goes towards her]

MOTHER.   Oh, fucking Jesus, they are going to throw her in a heap!

BIANCA.   Run, then, and save me! [THE MOTHER staggers towards the door, meeting LEANTIO]

MOTHER.   Oh, son, I thought you had a fort.... [She turns back] I won't go, dear. I think they'll throttle me. And I've never seen this done....

BIANCA [to LIVIA].   You are a woman. Intervene!

LIVIA.   No, sweet and perfumed thing, we have the same sex, but are not equally women. It's a false sisterhood you seek in me.

BIANCA.   Oh, utter vileness to wreck this wedding....

SORDIDO.   No, this is the proper matrimony! The people marry you! [He seizes her]

LEANTIO.   Oh, dear girl wife, who clung to me in perfect innocence, in shadows of her father's well —

LIVIA.   **It is not her.**

LEANTIO.   I hate this life which wrings such changes!   [He weeps on LIVIA] Give me the lie of innocence, always the lie —

LIVIA.   No, life is alteration, the shedding of all things until at death there's no regret, but all's been spent, discard, discard or petrify! [ISABELLA runs off] Stop her!

SORDIDO [emerging].   Is that love? Is that?

MOTHER.   Search me what love is, son.....

SORDIDO.   **I say it is.**

MOTHER.   It is, then....

SORDIDO [to LIVIA].   She loves me....

LIVIA [seeing his madness].   Yes....

SORDIDO.   **Does I say.** [He looks around] She is a miracle, beneath. It was as if I knew her, and always had. I could die now, and not protest....

THE DUKE, HIPPOLITO, THE CARDINAL burst in armed.

DUKE.   Oh, my property! They stamp about my loveliness! Look, her clothes cling round his boots! Die, you thing of shit and sewerage! [He kills SORDIDO] I am defiled! [HIPPOLITO goes to attack LIVIA] Not her! keep her for torture! Dogs to lick her womb!

ISABELLA.   Bianca! Where is Bianca!

DUKE.   See to her, I cannot...cannot come near such a pitch of muddy squalor as my bride is now....

CARDINAL.   Can she stand? Or is she injured?

DUKE.   **I don't know I haven't looked.** [He sees LEANTIO] You, I understand. So when you die I'll think, through all his twitching, as the skin peels off his flesh, he gloats to know he wounded me, his enemy.... [To LIVIA] But you, envious and unwomanly, such a refinement of horror as you deserve will tax the most senior torturer's imagination.   I'll send to Turkey, or to China, for the pain that suits you best....

LEANTIO.   Mother, even you will suffer....

MOTHER.   Me? I've got no politics.

CARDINAL.   The blind man also feels the storm.

MOTHER.   **I only came 'ere for a decent dinner.**

DUKE [to ISABELLA, who is attending BIANCA].   How is she? She must go through with it, or government is mocked. Sentries are fainting in the heat and mobs of dirty unemployed press on one anothers' backs. She must go through with it!

HIPPOLITO.   All who've witnessed this, kill off. And what's not known will start no rumour.

DUKE [seeing BIANCA, staggering].   Oh, my shame and my —

BIANCA [seeing SORDIDO's body].   You stabbed him...

DUKE.   **I slew the thief.**   [He extends a hand to her]   You are not damaged?

BIANCA.   Damaged....

DUKE.   You seem — ruffled but — not imperfect....

BIANCA.   Imperfect? I — [She shudders, falls into THE DUKE's arms]

HIPPOLITO.   Press her...!   Tell her, on her own two feet. Her coach is squealing on its springs and you should be at the cathedral.

BIANCA.   No —

DUKE.   Be sweet now, you are not so very —

BIANCA.   Not so very, no —

DUKE.   Some spirit for her, to bring back colour in her cheeks — look, the bastard scratched her — **Powder it!**   [He turns away, in disgust]

BIANCA [as HIPPOLITO comes to examine her].   **Don't touch.**   [She fingers the place]   Why did he? Was I too beautiful for him? I think he would have snapped my spine, my loveliness enraged him so. Did he hate beauty?

LIVIA.   Yes, to see it sell itself —

DUKE.   **Powder her cheek.**   We are too late already —

BIANCA.   No. [Pause. He stares at her]   No.

DUKE.   I would remind you, lovely as you are —

BIANCA.   Are? Liar. You mean were.

DUKE.   I would remind you, lovely as you —

BIANCA.   **Were** —

DUKE.   You are not flesh alone but also state, as I am, also **State.**

BIANCA.   You did not mention that behind the statues, I thought you then pure male but now I find —

DUKE.   **Mention it? You knew it, hypocrite!**   The rod that thrust between your skirts was double thick with wealth and treble thick with power, you flowed for it! [Pause]

BIANCA.   Yes...and that's not love, is it?   Is it?   [She looks at THE CARDINAL]   Oh, what am I, then? When I go — when I tremble for a man, for this man and not for that one, what is it made of, love?

CARDINAL.   A discourse on the origins of passion I more than most, would dearly love to hear deliberated, but in the street all Florence wonders what —

BIANCA.   Oh, fuck Florence.... [She smiles]   Well, of course, I have.... [She goes to LIVIA]   Dear woman, your eyes are gates damming back the torrents in your soul.... [LIVIA holds her]   I forgive you...the selling of me to this merchant of men...and I forgive you twice...the undoing of my knotted womb which swelled and gushed to base desire.... [to DUKE ETC]   I'll not act the coronation. [She holds LIVIA]

HIPPOLITO.   This is real shit we're plunged in.

DUKE.   Shut up.

HIPPOLITO.   I tell you, we —

DUKE.   Do up your gob, you quivering bastard!

HIPPOLITO.   Ridicule can topple empires....

DUKE.   I do so hate — at moments of the deepest crisis — clever dicks delivering homilies!   [He walks a little, stops]   I ask her once again, and if she won't must stab her and say the violator did it. So I'll convert this farce into a tragedy, and win more pity than contempt. I'll be the black-clad mourner of all Europe, and all future cruelty will be explained away by pain.

HIPPOLITO [in awe].   Oh, God, the brilliance of him...!

CARDINAL [aghast].   But she — her beauty — she is so —
DUKE.   Oh, he trembles at the well of love! On your knees to her spoiled
    fundament! [He thrusts THE CARDINAL aside] Bianca, adored woman and
    picture of purity, come now and kneel in sight of all and seal our love.
    [He extends a hand. Aside to MOTHER] Get pins, do up her garments.
    [Pause. BIANCA does not respond] Never mind the love, then. Kneel
    anyway. [His hand remains] Come on, we had incredible nights and will
    again. [Pause. She still refuses] **No act that two could do was not
    attempted by us, What is this!** [Weeping, he turns to THE CARDINAL] Oh,
    on her funeral, my weeping will be real, I shall go naked through the
    streets behind her coffin....
BIANCA.   I must be truthful. In cunt. If nowhere else, then there. For
    all the lies we carry, and must carry, lies of politics and kindness, the
    small lie and the big, I don't protest. All the things we handle leave us
    stained, but there I do want — **Futile pursuit, who knows** — I do want
    truth. Not hungering for what my father tutored me was male, or nurses
    giggling at the soldiers' strut, but what my stripped emotion commands
    me. And him, utterly anonymous on the floor, did break some bond, for if
    I loved power, and power was my dream of male, he had it, too. **Help me
    understand my needs.** [Pause. They stare at her]
DUKE.   Yes, will do, and work it out at leisure in our villa, dwarfs and
    maniacs if that's your craving....
BIANCA.   Oh, God, I never felt so cold, such a deep cold and so alone....
    [She goes to disrobe] Get these clinging weapons off me and I'll wander.
DUKE.   **Wander? Wander!** Never wander! You have fucked your entrance
    into politics, never wander more, you are collared for your lust!
CARDINAL.   They are frothing in the streets, and turning over toffee apple
    stalls....
DUKE.   Wander, no.... [He puts his hand to his dagger] Forgive me, Lord
    of Governments, who lends His mercy to him stretched between love and
    responsibility.... [He goes towards BIANCA]
LIVIA.   Don't kill her for confusing your costume with your sex....
DUKE [striking her].   **Hate! Hate the knowing woman!** [He stares at
    her]
HIPPOLITO.   Act then.... [THE DUKE turns to BIANCA] Act... [Pause.
    LEANTIO goes to move, but LIVIA restrains him]
LEANTIO.   Oh, my life's love....
HIPPOLITO.   Act, or the market will be trampled and money bleed to
    death...!
CARDINAL.   I think, if Christ stood here, his wounds would open to hear
    money made your god...!
HIPPOLITO.   **Act!**
DUKE [touching BIANCA's exposed neck].   Oh, this perfect neck all white
    with cruelty, it rots — all — calculation — Bianca...!   [He slides
    down her, to his knees, sobbing]
HIPPOLITO.   Oh, somebody govern! [He goes to take the dagger from THE
    DUKE, but THE WARD enters]
WARD.   No rush.... [He goes to the body of SORDIDO]   Beloved,
    uncharitable thing. If every stab was gob what a roar of derision would
    thunder out your corpse! **Do you think it hurt him to be killed?** He
    hated life, it was absurd to him. His sneering lip! He flung words like
    shards of glass against the flashy whore and schoolgirls blushing with
    false innocence, monarchs, tramps, all their posturing he slashed.   I
    shall be so alone....
HIPPOLITO [inspired].   Govern the state.
WARD.   Why? You take me for a cynic, and therefore fit to rule? I'd no
    more force decisions on the rest than throttle babies in their prams,
    which I considered once, for humour.... [He looks at LIVIA] Let her.
HIPPOLITO.   Her? She's been seen skirts-up in the alley.
WARD.   Good. Let her govern. She knows, and she hates money. Let that be
    your manifesto! **I love and I hate money.** Quote it, publish now!
HIPPOLITO [pursuing his intuition].   You, for all your mockery, you have
    the wisdom, think!
WARD.   I am too good an actor. I would tell the truth in such a way to

make it unbelievable, and then they'd all rejoice to swallow simple lies! No, she is the fittest for a dynasty.

HIPPOLITO [hurrying away].   Oh, catastrophe.

BIANCA.   Is also birth....

CARDINAL.   What?

BIANCA.   Catastrophe is also birth. Out the ruins crawls the bloody thing, unrecognizable in the ripped rags of former life.   Ghastly breaths of unfamiliar air!   Like the infant, expelled from the silent womb, screams red its horror, then tastes oxygen. I have to find my life! [LIVIA goes to embrace her] **Don't touch.** [She freezes] Too new to be suffocated by your impulsive sisterhood.   I'll bruise.   I'll crush in your embrace....

MOTHER [staggering].   Take me, someone!

LEANTIO.   Oh, you waddling bag of rheumatism and sinking flesh, can't you get enough of life? [THE WARD tugs her away, then stops, seeing ISABELLA]

WARD.   Isabella? What of you, then? [She does not reply, but goes to BIANCA, stands by her] Isabella? [She does not reply. He goes out. There is a cacophony of running feet, yells off. THE CARDINAL goes to make his escape]

LIVIA [seeing him].   Get Christ out of your pocket. He knew money strangled love, and love's corpse stifled imagination, and dead imagination was the ground from which more money grew. Money, death, and money! [He starts to go] **Don't go.**

CARDINAL [turning violently on her].   Love! To hear you speak of love who engineered this agony! **Murder of words.** [He goes out. LIVIA reaches a hand to LEANTIO]

LIVIA.   Leantio, down to the street now. And tell the people we have broken lies and tread the pieces. [He stares at her] Leantio...down to the street now and —

LEANTIO.   **Stay by her.** [He looks at BIANCA] Must....

BIANCA.   I do not want it, Leantio. Little spasm of male pity. Male violence, male pity. The blow. The charity. Get off...!

ISABELLA.   Escape, or we shall never!

LIVIA.   Rags, tattered trousseau in the alleys, run! [Suddenly BIANCA strikes LIVIA in the face. LIVIA reels, as does BIANCA from the force of it. Pause]

BIANCA.   Thank you....   [They stare at one another, then ISABELLA hurries BIANCA away. Pause, LIVIA, LEANTIO apart and still]

DUKE.   New duke! [He points to LEANTIO] New duchess! [He points to LIVIA. LIVIA and LEANTIO go to hurry out] Don't love...! Don't love...!